Poitiers 1356

The capture of a king

OSPREY
PUBLISHING

Poitiers 1356

The capture of a king

David Nicolle • Illustrated by Graham Turner

Series editor Lee Johnson • Consultant editor David G Chandler

First published in Great Britain in 2004 by Osprey Publishing, Elms Court, Chapel Way, Botley, Oxford OX2 9LP, United Kingdom. Email: info@ospreypublishing.com

A CIP catalogue record for this book is available from the British Library

ISBN 1 84176 516 3

Editor: Lee Johnson
Design: The Black Spot
Index by Alan Thatcher
Maps by The Map Studio
3D bird's-eye views by The Black Spot
Battlescene artwork by Graham Turner
Originated by Grasmere Digital Imaging, Leeds, UK
Printed in China through World Print Ltd.

04 05 06 07 08   10 9 8 7 6 5 4 3 2 1

For a catalogue of all books published by Osprey Military and Aviation please contact:

Osprey Direct UK, P.O. Box 140, Wellingborough, Northants, NN8 2FA, UK
E-mail: info@ospreydirect.co.uk

Osprey Direct USA, c/o MBI Publishing, P.O. Box 1, 729 Prospect Ave, Osceola, WI 54020, USA
E-mail: info@ospreydirectusa.com

www.ospreypublishing.com

Dedication

This one is for my late father, a great fan of Froissart.

Artist's note

Readers may care to note that the original paintings from which the colour plates in this book were prepared are available for private sale. All reproduction copyright whatsoever is retained by the Publishers. All enquiries should be addressed to:

Graham Turner
'Five Acres'
Buslins Lane
Chartridge, Chesham,
Bucks, HP5 2SN
UK

The Publishers regret that they can enter into no correspondence upon this matter.

KEY TO MILITARY SYMBOLS

CONTENTS

FRANCE FROM THE BATTLE OF CRÉCY (1346) TO 1355

Spread of the 'Black Death' plague.
French and allied operations.
English and allied operations.

● Castles and towns retaken by French royal forces from the English and their allies (1349–50).

● English garrisons installed in Quercy, though most of the main towns remained under French royal control (1351–52).

■ Towns taken or retaken by English forces (December 1355 to February 1356).

Dec 1349: Raid by Henry of Grosmont, Earl (subsequently Duke) of Lancaster, into Languedoc.

Oct–Dec 1355: Great Raid by Prince Edward of Wales (the Black Prince) into Languedoc.

English conquests in south-western France.

The Kingdom of France in 1355.
French territory under English rule in 1346.
Territory acquired by the Crown of France (with date).
Imperial frontier territory ruled by French feudal lords.
Territory outside France under French rulers.
Kingdom of England in 1355.
Papal territory of Avignon, within the Kingdom of France.
Béarn (declared an independent sovereign state in 1347).

ENGLAND

London

Nov 1355: Abortive raid by English under King Edward III from Calais.

Bruges
Ghent
Calais
FLANDERS   'IMPERIAL' FLANDERS
Lille   'THE THREE CASTLERIES'
ARTOIS
PONTHIEU
Cambrai

November 1355: French countermove from Amiens.
Amiens

PICARDY

N

Rouen
ILE DE FRANCE
Reims
Paris

THE EMPIRE

English Channel

Guernsey
Jersey
Carentan

NORMANDY
Argentan

CHAMPAGNE   BAR

Brest

BRITTANY

MAINE
Chartres
Le Mans
ORLÉANAIS
Orléans

Troyes

Rennes

1349–50: French offensives under Guy de Nesle, Le Gallois de la Heuse and Fulk de Laval against English and allied garrisons.

Nantes   Angers
ANJOU

Tours
TOURAINE

Bourges
BERRY
Nevers
NIVERNAIS

BURGUNDY (French Duchy)
Dijon

POITOU   Poitiers

Bourbon
BOURBONNAIS

BURGUNDY (Imperial County)
Mâcon

SAVOY

Bay of Biscay

La Rochelle
ANGOUMOIS
MARCHE

1349–50: Castilian fleet in support of the French.

Saintes
SAINTONGE   Angoulême
Limoges
LIMOUSIN

AUVERGNE   LYONNAIS
Lyons

VELAY/
St Flour   Le Puy

DAUPHINÉ (1349)

PÉRIGORD   Périgueux

Bordeaux

GUYENNE

GASCONY

QUERCY   ROUERGUE   GEVAUDAN

VALENCE

ARMAGNAC

AGENAIS

ASTARAC
BÉARN
SOULE
BIGORRE
COMINGES

Toulouse

LANGUEDOC
Montpellier (1349)

Avignon
Arles

PROVENCE

Marseilles

CASTILE

FOIX

Narbonne

Mediterranean Sea

NAVARRE

ROUSSILLON

ARAGON

0   100 miles
0   100 km

INTRODUCTION

Throughout most of the Middle Ages, French and English societies were very similar, especially in the heartlands of southern England and northern France. Furthermore the ruling class of England still spoke French and were largely of French origin. In contrast there were noticeable differences in speech, culture and law from southern France with its significant Romano-Mediterranean heritage. So it was ironic that the English Crown's most extensive French estates and most loyal French allies were in Aquitaine, in south-western France, which, though not Mediterranean, had preserved its Romano-Christian civilisation throughout the early medieval period.

The first decade of what came to be known as the Hundred Years War between France and England saw two remarkable English victories. The first was at sea, near the port of Sluys in 1340. The second was even more surprising to other European observers, being King Edward III's crushing defeat of King Philip VI at the battle of Crécy (see Campaign 71: *Crécy 1346 – Triumph of the Longbow*). Suddenly a kingdom that had been noted for peace and prosperity rather than military prowess earned a reputation as a source of highly effective armies and of increasingly respected longbow archers.

Two years after Crécy, France suffered an even greater catastrophe with the arrival of the Black Death – an outbreak of bubonic plague that soon spread across almost all of Europe, but which apparently entered France through the thriving Mediterranean port of Marseilles. Millions died during several waves of epidemics and some historians maintain that

'Noble men and women at play', on an early to mid-14th-century French carved ivory panel. The game on the left was known as Hot Cockles. Before the outbreak of the Hundred Years War, the French aristocracy, their culture and way of life, were admired and imitated throughout western Europe, including England. (Musée du Louvre, Paris)

up to half the population of France may have succumbed. Not surprisingly, the Black Death brought campaigning between England and France to a virtual standstill. The plague even had an impact on the availability of horses because a collapse of the rural economy and rural population meant that insufficient fodder could be found to keep large horse-herds alive. Such factors were important because, by the mid-14th century, the Hundred Years War was an economic as well as military struggle that imposed severe financial strain on both sides.

When John II came to the throne of France in 1350 he inherited a kingdom weakened by disease, famine and a series of wide-ranging English *chevauchée* raids. The young king ruled with the support of a small group of senior barons and representatives of the lesser aristocracy. Their consent was needed before such things as new taxation. The most powerful lords normally met their king within their own geopolitical power-bases, and nothing like the English parliamentary House of Lords had yet developed. On the other hand King John II made strenuous efforts to reform the government, consolidate royal power and strengthen France's armies in the wake of their defeats by the once despised English. To keep control of his newly reformed government structure, John II abandoned the roving lifestyle of his father Philip and spent most of his time in or near Paris. He also selected three *Prelates* from the aristocracy to serve as military leaders and help carry out organisational reforms during a prolonged truce with England. Not all King John's policies were well thought out, however, and in 1352 he gave his daughter in marriage to King Charles of Navarre – known to history as Charles the Bad. This would cause serious problems in the future since Charles of Navarre already believed he should be King of France.

By 1355 the worst outbreaks of plague had passed and a recovery was under way. Yet the armies that France fielded in the 1350s were considerably smaller than the one that had fought at Crécy. Given King John II's reforms, these smaller armies should have been more efficient. For example, in 1351 the king ordered that every crossbowman in his service be supplied with one belt or spanning-strap and hooks proportionate to his strength and physical size. Elsewhere, traditional forms of urban defence had been neglected in the decades of peace before the Hundred Years War, especially in Poitou, where the great English raid of 1356 culminated in the battle of Poitiers. By then considerable efforts had been made to revive and improve the system of *guet*, *arrière-guet* and *garde* in cities and towns. In Châtellerault, for example, a *guetteur* or 'observer' was nominated by the town council to keep watch from the bell-tower of St Jacques. Sadly these efforts proved too slow and ineffective to have much impact in 1356. Attempts to strength urban fortifications and castles had similarly little effect and many historians blame the failure of King John's reforms on the supposed 'disloyalty' of the aristocratic elite, with their selfish defence of vested interests, their factionalism and indiscipline.

Meanwhile in England there had been fewer attempts at reform since English arms had already demonstrated their effectiveness. In fact King Edward's early successes were seen by many as evidence of divine support

'Burying the dead at Tournai during the Black Death, 1348', as illustrated in a history of the northern French city, now in Belgium, written by the local Abbot. France and England were both still suffering from the after-effects of the great plague when the Hundred Years War broke out again in 1355. (*Annales de Tournai par Gilis li Muisit*, Bibliothèque Royale, Brussels)

for his cause. After the battle of Crécy, John Erghome of Yorkshire wrote: *The Lord God ordains the English to have strength of arms and battles against the French on account of the rights which they have in the Kingdom of France.* Nevertheless there was widespread concern after Crécy that the French would cheat England of the spoils of victory through clever truces, treaties and devious diplomacy. There was also a growing suspicion that the Papacy was pro-French. Along with this went fear of French retaliation, since France had for so long been the greater power.

The traditional view that England profited from its early victories has recently been challenged, at least where the English government was concerned, since the costs of major expeditions remained huge. Nevertheless, individuals certainly profited from a successful campaign. Although medieval armies were tiny by modern standards, so were medieval populations, and the numbers of men involved were sometimes comparable to a modern mobilisation of 10 or even 15 per cent of suitably aged available manpower. Furthermore the idea that English armies lived off the land and that therefore 'France paid' is misleading. Major military expeditions involved huge amounts of food, animals, fodder and transport. Nor were the men involved in such campaigns merely the unwanted or undesirable elements. On the contrary, they included some of the most productive people. Lords lost many of their tenants and some of their retainers – permanently if they were killed. The cost for the losing side was even greater. Even when men survived, ransoms for those taken captive could permanently ruin families.

'St George' as shown in an early 14th-century English stained-glass window. George came to be recognised as the patron saint of England during the Hundred Years War with France. The simple arms and armour the saint wears here would still have been used by many non-elite troops on both sides during the battle of Poitiers. (*in situ* parish church, Brinsop, Herefordshire; author's photograph)

One major gain for England, during the first phase of the Hundred Years War, was its occupation of Calais in 1347. This gave the English domination of the Straits of Dover, and to consolidate this gain the port was repopulated with English settlers. French naval raiding of the English coast declined and would not revive until the 1370s, though there were still some attacks. Equally important was the relative security that English shipping enjoyed to and from Aquitaine. This would survive until Castilian galley fleets arrived in the English Channel as allies of France.

When major military operations resumed in 1355, the English continued their previous strategy of widespread raiding; Normandy, Brittany and French-ruled parts of Aquitaine suffering as a result. While King Edward III of England summoned his Parliament, King John II assembled the *États Generaux*, or States General, in his palace. On 1 September 1355 the French King ordered a general mobilisation and for ten months his armies achieved several minor victories. On the English side, three large-scale *chevauchée* raids were launched, but only one could be considered successful. King Edward III's *chevauchée* from Calais was a failure, while that led by the Duke of Lancaster in Normandy similarly achieved little because negotiations with Charles of Navarre broke down.

In contrast, Prince Edward of Wales' march from Bordeaux on the Atlantic coast of France to Narbonne on its Mediterranean shore inflicted huge damage. The Treaty of Valonges, on 10 September 1355, had marked a reconciliation between King John II France and King Charles of Navarre. This was seen as a threat to English interests and so Edward III ordered his son, Prince Edward of Wales – soon to be known as the Black Prince – to launch a great *chevauchée* through the lands of Jean d'Armagnac, a key supporter of King John II in south-western France. Before this expedition the King of England summoned Parliament where, according to the Chandos Herald: *All were of accord likewise to send the Prince into Gascony, because he was of such renown, and ordained forthwith that with him should go the noble Earl of Warwick, of high esteem, and the Earl of Salisbury, of great valiance, the gallant Earl of Suffolk, Ufford was his name, and the Earl of Oxford, the good Earl of Stafford, Sir Bartholomew de Burghersh, bold in deed, Sir John of Montagu, proud and impetuous, the Lord of Despencer, and Basset of high renown; and there was also the Lord of Mohun, and likewise, the good Reginald Cobham, who had been in many an assault; there was also Chandos and Audley; these two were of great renown and were appointed chief advisors.*[1] Most of these men would subsequently feature prominently at the battle of Poitiers. The Chandos Herald's description of their departure from Plymouth has a contemporary ring, though couched in archaic language: *Right sore greaved were they at heart when it came to his departing, for there you might see lady and damsel weep and make moan in complaints; the one wept for her husband, the other lamented for her lover.*

'Citizens and soldiers watch as Jews are burned at Tournai during the Black Death, 1348', as illustrated in a history by the local Abbot. Jews and other minorities were widely blamed for causing or spreading the plague, though they themselves clearly suffered from the disease to the same degree as their Christian neighbours. (*Annales de Tournai par Gilis li Muisit*, Bibliothèque Royale, Brussels)

In late September 1355, 1,000 men-at-arms, 1,000 horses, 300–400 infantry archers and 170 Welsh spearmen sailed from Plymouth. The Prince had also 'indentured' with King Edward for 433 men-at-arms, 400 mounted and 300 infantry archers, needing at least 833 horses, plus horses for the leaders, their retinues, and certain essential administrative staff, not to mention carts and baggage animals. Some men-at-arms were allowed to buy horses in Gascony and replacements for animals lost in service might also be found there; all to be valued by the *Constable* of Bordeaux. Those horses shipped directly from Plymouth were 'appraised' (valued) and marked by a certain John Geyncourt and his assistants, while two farriers sailed with the army and Lambkyn Saddler supplied some of the Prince's own horse-harness.

Because other suitable military supplies were limited in Aquitaine, much was sent from England. According to the 'Register' or official documents of the Black Prince, Robert Pipot of Broukford was sent back to England; *to buy and purvey for his use a thousand bows, two thousand sheaves of arrows and four hundred gross of bowstrings, but no arrows can be obtained from England because the King* [Edward III] *has caused to be arrested and taken for his use all the arrows that can be found anywhere there, so that the Prince is now sending the said Robert to the parts of Chester to arrest the fletchers* [arrow-makers] *themselves to continue working at their craft for the Prince until his need is satisfied.*[2] The Prince also sent men to Lincoln for bows and arrows, and to Cornwall for horses for his mounted archers.

When the Black Prince reached Bordeaux in 1355, several important local lords came to meet him; *To him came incontinent the noble Prince d'Albret*

and the valiant and doughty Lord of Montferrat, Mussidan, Roson, Curton and Amenieu de Fossard, and the great Lord of Pommiers and many noble knights, and the rightful Lord of Lesparre.[3] As a result, when the Prince's army set out on 5 October they were joined by many Gascon troops including the Captal de Buch. The subsequent *chevauchée* was a remarkable achievement, marching over 1,100 kilometres (684 miles) from Bordeaux to Narbonne and back. Prince Edward even considered attacking Toulouse but this proved too difficult without a proper siege train.

Instead the Prince crossed the rushing Garonne and Ariège rivers then pressed on eastward into previously untouched areas where his raiders caused huge damage. Even the suburbs of Carcassonne were burned, though the fortified *cité* or citadel could not be taken. The same happened at Narbonne where the resistance of the *cité* persuaded the Prince that it was time to retreat. His army executed the retreat successfully, despite heavy rain, muddy roads, and the flooded Garonne, which they again crossed safely.

Over 500 settlements, villages and towns are believed to have been burned during the Black Prince's *chevauchée* of 1355, and the campaign was a catastrophe for the Languedoc region of southern France, coming so soon after the Black Death. Furthermore French forces had been weakened by arguments between the Count of Armagnac and King John's *Constable* in the area, rendering them unable to resist the Anglo-Gascon *chevauchée*. On the other hand the Black Prince's army lost many horses; this being blamed upon the great distances covered. In reality the high attrition rate was probably because the animals had been insufficiently rested after arriving from England and consequently died of 'shipping fever' or 'strangles'.

After his Narbonne raid, the Black Prince wintered at Bordeaux and quartered troops at the *bastides*, or fortified towns, of La Réole, Sainte-Foy, Saint-Emilion and around Libourne. The Captal de Buch, Chandos and Audley spent the winter partly in open camp and partly skirmishing further afield for lodging around the French towns of Agen, Cahors and Porte Sainte-Marie. They even attacked the castle of Périgueux.

In response, French forces used the winter of 1355/56 successfully, retaking over 30 towns and castles. However, news that the French king was raising money for a great army to march against the English resulted in a drastic devaluation of the French currency. Worse was to follow for King John II when he again quarrelled with King Charles of Navarre and, in April 1356, had him arrested for treason. As well as being king of Navarre, Charles was a senior member of the French aristocracy and held huge lands within France. As result Charles' brother Philip of Navarre formed an alliance with King Edward III of England. This opened up strategic possibilities for the English not only in south-western France but also in the north where Philip held large estates. These could now be attacked by the French King in response to Philip's alliance with the enemy, while the English had an excuse for 'relieving' Philip of Navarre's now threatened estates.

The waterfront in the city of Bergerac on the river Dordogne. In the 14th century Bergerac was an important river port linking the eastern parts of English-ruled Aquitaine with Bordeaux, the Atlantic and England. It was from here that the Black Prince's army set out on their great raid early in August 1356. (Fred Nicolle photograph)

In January 1356 the Black Prince sent raids to maintain pressure on the French around Aquitaine. The Earl of Warwick was active in the Garonne valley, moving upstream from La Réole to seize Tonneins and Clairac. The Earls of Suffolk, Oxford and Salisbury led a raid towards Notre Dame de Rocamadour, while Bartholomew de Burghersh raided as far as Cognac and Saintonge. The Captal de Buch was active in this same area, installing garrisons at Rochefort, Tonnay and Taillebourg.

Chandos and Audley then left Libourne for the Garonne valley and reached Agen, which was defended by Jean d'Armagnac himself. However, the French commander stayed inside the fortified town while the English ravaged the surroundings then raided Cahors and Porte Sainte-Marie before heading north to Périgord. Here the Count of Périgord feared an assault and asked his brother, Cardinal Talleyrand, to get the Pope to persuade the English to leave his city alone. The Black Prince was offered a lot of money but refused, saying that his job was to punish those who had 'rebelled' against his father's authority in Aquitaine. Périgueux was then captured by the Captal de Buch and a large garrison installed before the Captal went on to take several places in the eastern Saintonge area.

The list of places seized by the English during this period was long and by May 1356 over 30 towns and castles, which had in earlier times been part of the Angevin 'empire' in Aquitaine, were 'recovered' for the English Crown. Equally significantly, Prince Edward won back the allegiance of many Gascon lords, usually with offers of money or lands. These lords

'The Archangel St Michael' in the *Book of Hours of Joan of Navarre*, French, c.1336. It is interesting to note that the Archangel has been given a shield bearing the red cross normally associated with St George. Below, a varlet is seen armed with a bow. (*Heures de Jeanne de Navarre*, Bibliothèque Nationale, Ms. Nouv. Acq. Latin 3145, f. 184, Paris)

subsequently provided men for the *chevauchée* that culminated in the battle of Poitiers. Most important was the attachment of several lords along the north-west frontier of the English-ruled zone. Here men like Durfort, Caumont, Galard and D'Albret could be seen as political weathervanes, indicating the attitudes and sympathies of the local Gascon aristocracy. Nevertheless the French still held several garrisons west of the Garonne river, deep inside territory that was otherwise dominated by English or pro-English forces.

Further reinforcements were requested from England early in 1356, as indicated in a surviving Royal letter that instructed the Lieutenant of the Justice and the Chamberlain of Chester: *… insomuch as the King has ordered that three hundred archers be sent speedily to the Prince in Gascony in the company of Sir Richard de Stafford, and wills that two hundred of them be from the country of Chester and the remainder from elsewhere as ordered, to cause two hundred of the best mounted archers they can find to be chosen, selected and arrayed with all possible speed in the said county, appoint two suitable persons of the said country to be their leaders …*[4] Ten days later another order demanded that 300 further archers be added to this number. Elsewhere recruitment for the Black Prince's 1356 expedition drew in men from Westmoreland, Yorkshire and even from Germany.

In early spring 1356 new horses were ordered for the Prince's army. Sumpters or packhorses were purchased and the Prince's 'receivers' in Cornwall were ordered to buy 30 of the strongest baggage animals available, as well as providing 30 grooms. The Earls of Warwick, Suffolk, Salisbury, Oxford and Stafford similarly had fresh mounts sent from England in two transport ships that had been set aside for their animals and food. Meanwhile animals and victuals were being raised for the Duke of Lancaster's campaign in Normandy, so England's horse and agriculture resources were clearly being stretched to the limit.

1 Chandos Herald, *Life of the Black Prince by the Herald of Sir John Chandos*, ed. & trans. M.K. Pope and E.C. Lodge (Oxford, 1910) pp. 139–140.
2 In B. Emerson, *The Black Prince* (London, 1976) pp. 102–3.
3 Chandos Herald, *loc. cit.*
4 From the Register of the Black Prince, in B. Emerson, *op. cit*, 102.

CHRONOLOGY

1347

Béarn declared by Count Gaston Phoebus of Foix to be an independent sovereign state; this not recognised by the King of France. 'Black Death' plague reaches Marseilles.

1349

Dauphiné purchased from the Empire; Montpellier gained from Aragon.
December Raid by Duke of Lancaster into Languedoc reaches Toulouse but is obliged to retreat.

1349–50

French retake Prigny, Bouin, Beauvoir and Noirmoutier in southern Brittany from the English and their allies.

1351–52

English garrisons installed in the province of Quercy, although most of the main towns remain under French control.

1355

October–December Great Raid by Prince Edward of Wales into Languedoc reaches Narbonne.
November Abortive raid by King Edward III from Calais reaches Hesdin but retreats when confronted by French troops from Amiens.
December (to February 1356) Several towns taken by English in the provinces of Périgord, Guyenne and Agenais.

1356

June Assembly of urban representatives of Languedoc at Béziers to coordinate their defences.
19 June Earl of Stafford brings reinforcements and orders from King Edward to the Black Prince in Bordeaux.
21 June Papal peace delegation leaves Avignon, heading for the French court.
June–July Raid by Duke of Lancaster across Normandy.
July Southampton declared point of embarkation for expeditionary force to France. King John II sends the Count of Poitiers to Bourges to assemble an army; *arrière-ban* is proclaimed with men to assemble by 1 August.
6 July Prince of Wales moves to La Réole, which is assembly point for Gascon forces.
12 July King John besieges Bréteuil.
Early August Aragonese fleet arrives at the river Seine; Count of Poitiers establishes his HQ at Bourges.
August (and early September) Advance by Duke of Lancaster, in support of the Prince of Wales.
4 August Prince Edward's army reaches Bergerac and divides, with a small force left to defend Gascony.
9 August Prince Edward reaches Brantôme.

'Knights in combat', illustrated in an English *Psalter* from the early to mid-14th century. This sort of arms, armour and horse-harness would have been common at Poitiers. (*The Ormesby Psalter*, Bodleian Library, Ms. Douce 366, f. 54r, Oxford)

10 August Aragonese fleet stops reinforcements leaving Southampton for France.

12 August Prince Edward reaches Rochechouart.

18 August Count of Poitiers withdraws from Bourges; establishes new HQ at Decise by **21 August**; is ordered to hold the Loire until the King and the Dauphin join him.

19 August Prince Edward reaches Lussac.

20 August Navarrese garrison at Bréteuil surrenders the castle to King John.

22 August Prince Edward reaches Argenton.

Last week of August King John sends Marshal Jean de Clermont to defend the Touraine; reconnaissance forces are sent south of the Loire to harass Prince Edward; King John moves to Chartres where he reorganises his army.

23 August Prince Edward reaches Châteauroux.

24 August Prince Edward reaches Issoudun.

26 August Gascon force under the Captal de Buch sacks Vierzon.

28 August English advance force defeats a troop of French men-at-arms but fails to find a crossing point over the Loire; Prince Edward reaches Vierzon.

29 August Captal de Buch captures a French scouting party.

31 August–3 September English take Romorantin.

5 September Prince Edward marches along the north bank of the Cher.

7 September Prince Edward reaches Tours and establishes his HQ at Montlouis; English assault on Tours is defeated.

8 September King John's army reaches Meung-sur-Loire.

10 September King John joins forces with the Count of Poitiers, crosses the Loire and marches to Amboise.

11 September Prince Edward retreats south, crossing the Cher and Indre to reach Montbazon.

12 September Papal peace delegation meets Prince Edward. French forces under the Dauphin Charles reach Tours around this date; King John marches from Amboise towards Poitiers.

13 September Prince Edward reaches La Haye on the Creuse. King John reaches Loches.

14 September King John reaches La Haye. Prince Edward reaches Châtellerault and remains three days hoping to make contact with the Duke of Lancaster, who is unable to cross the Loire.

15 September King John reaches Chauvigny.

17 September Prince Edward leaves Châtellerault, marches through the forests between the Clain and Vienne. He reaches the Chauvigny–Poitiers road to find that the French are already heading for Poitiers; Captal de Buch attacks the French rearguard at La Chaboterie; English withdraw and make camp in the forest.

18 September English find the French camped between Poitiers and Savigny-Lévescault; Prince Edward arrays his army for battle north of Nouaillé.

19 September Battle of Poitiers Prince Edward defeats and captures King John II.

21 September Anglo-Gascon army marches south from Poitiers.

29 September Dauphin Charles enters Paris to establish a new French government.

Late September Duke of Lancaster withdraws to Brittany.

3 October The English and their Breton supporters unsuccessfully besiege Rennes.

October (to January 1358) Anglo-Navarrese occupation of large parts of Normandy.

December Pont-Audemer retaken by the Dauphin Charles.

OPPOSING COMMANDERS

ENGLISH COMMANDERS

Edward the Black Prince was in overall command of the great raid or *chevauchée* that culminated in the battle of Poitiers. He was born at Woodstock on 13 June 1330, the eldest son of King Edward III of England and Queen Philippa of Hainault, was proclaimed Prince of Wales on 12 May 1343, and died at Westminster on 8 July 1376, a year before his father. As heir to the English throne he was loaded with symbolic duties from an early age, being Earl of Chester at age three and Duke of Cornwall at six. In 1338 the Prince was left as the symbolic 'guardian of the realm' during King Edward III's first invasion of France. His own involvement in the Hundred Years War began in 1345 and a year later Prince Edward 'won his spurs' at the battle of Crécy where he nominally commanded the English vanguard. His nickname of the Black Prince was probably earned during his ruthless *chevauchée* to Narbonne in 1355. However, the Black Prince really won military fame at the battle of Poitiers while his personal legend also benefited from his chivalrous treatment of the captured French king. Though praised by contemporaries as a 'perfect knight', the Prince's reputation for chivalry came from tournaments rather than warfare. He clearly lacked skill as a ruler in Aquitaine and never won the genuine support of the Gascon nobility. By 1370 the Black Prince was very ill and conducted his last campaign while being carried in a litter. It was his savage treatment of the conquered city of Limoges during this expedition that severely damaged his reputation. Nevertheless, the Black Prince's name was added to the 'cult of Heroes' that was so popular amongst the English and French knightly classes during the 15th century.

Senior noblemen commanded various divisions of the Black Prince's army during the 1356 campaign. One of these was **Thomas Beauchamp, Earl of Warwick**, who was born in 1313 or 1314. His first military experience had been in the Scottish wars of the late 1330s. Appointed Marshal of England in 1344–46, he fought at Crécy and the siege of Calais. In 1352 the Earl of Warwick became Admiral of the Fleet in south-western England, was Constable of the Black Prince's army 1355–56 and fought at Poitiers where he captured the Bishop of Sens. Thomas Beauchamp died of plague at Calais in 1369.

William Montague, Earl of Salisbury, was born in 1328 into a family that strongly supported King Edward III. William himself was knighted alongside Prince Edward at the start of the Crécy campaign. However, the young Earl's relations with the Prince were often strained, especially over the fate of Denbighshire where both had strong interests. Appointed Constable of the King's army in France, he joined the Black Prince in Aquitaine and played a leading role at the battle of Poitiers. In 1360 the

A very damaged mid- to late 14th century Italian wall painting showing the Count of Savoy and his Crusading army. The mountainous and poor regions of Savoy provided mercenary soldiers for many of its neighbours, including France. Savoyards were especially renowned as infantry. (*in situ*, a hall of the bishop's palace at Colle Val d'Elsa near Siena)

Earl of Salisbury helped negotiate the Treaty of Brétigny. During the English Peasants' Revolt he advised the young King Richard II. The Earl is sometimes said to have accidentally killed his own son in a tournament. In 1397 he was made Governor of Calais but died that same year.

Robert Ufford, Earl of Suffolk, was one of the most experienced English leaders during the Poitiers campaign. Born in 1298, he inherited his father's lands because his elder brother died. Admiral of the English fleet in 1337, he was taken prisoner three years later. After his ransom and release, Robert Ufford fought at Crécy, the siege of Calais and the naval battle off Winchelsea. He had worked closely with Prince Edward since 1337 and accompanied the Prince to Aquitaine. Suffolk was often entrusted with delicate diplomatic missions by King Edward III and the Black Prince. He died in 1369.

John de Vere, Earl of Oxford, was closely involved in English governmental affairs after returning from Compostella in 1332. He saw active service in Scotland and served in France during the first years of the Hundred Years War, fighting at Crécy, alongside the Black Prince in 1355 and was a senior advisor at the battle of Poitiers. The Earl of Oxford died during the siege of Reims in 1360.

Jean III de Grailly, the Captal de Buch, was the most noted Gascon commander of the Poitiers campaign. His family held extensive lands in the wine-making area of Médoc. He was the son of the elder Jean de Grailly and Blanche de Foix, and was a cousin of Count Gaston Phoebus of Foix. He inherited the title of Captal in 1343 and thus enjoyed many privileges in the *Parlement* of Bordeaux. He became the Black Prince's Lieutenant in Aquitaine and distinguished himself at the battle of Poitiers, being rewarded with the castle of Cognac as a result. After serving in Prussia as a Crusader, Jean de Grailly remained a loyal supporter of King Charles of Navarre and was involved in negotiating the treaty of Brétigny. The second time he was taken prisoner by French royal forces, King Charles V refused to free the Captal unless he swore never to take up arms against France again. Jean de Grailly refused and died, still a prisoner, in 1377.

FRENCH COMMANDERS

King John II, 'The Good'. Before becoming King, John II married Bonne of Bohemia, a daughter of the blind King of Bohemia who was killed at Crécy. She died of plague in 1349 however, the same year as John's mother. John was next engaged to Blanche d'Evreux, a daughter of the King of Navarre, but then John's father King Philip married the girl himself. Eventually Prince John married Blanche de Boulogne in 1350 and a few months later became king. John II soon earned a reputation for enjoying almost constant festivities and it was this, rather than any particular benefits

The old city of Angers and the river Mayenne viewed from the top of the early 13th-century castle. Angers was far too strong for the Duke of Lancaster to take in 1356 so his large raiding army marched further south to the banks of the river Loire, only a few kilometres away. There Lancaster was baulked by another island fortress at Les-Ponts-de-Cé. With a river in front of him he could not cross and the strongly garrisoned city of Angers to his rear, Lancaster was unable to advance in support of the Black Prince. (Author's photograph)

of his reign as King, which earned King John his nickname of 'The Good'. Some historians still regard John II as divorced from reality and see his reign as a disaster for France. However, the evidence suggests that King John II was not the punctilious fool of popular prejudice but seems to have been a sensitive patron of art and scholarship who strove to improve French government institutions and strengthen the royal army. His father's defeat by the English at Crécy did leave him with a low opinion of the French military aristocracy and as a result King John II tried not to rely on the senior nobility too much.

The King's eldest son, **the Dauphin** or **Crown Prince Charles** (the future King Charles V 'The Wise'), enjoys a much higher reputation. He married his cousin Jeanne de Bourbon in 1350 but also kept a mistress, Biette Cassinel, and is said to have worn her badge on his armour. In 1355 Charles was made Duke of Normandy, which is how he is described in most chronicles of the battle of Poitiers. After escaping from the battle, the Dauphin made his way to Paris where he would eventually prove to be one of the most successful rulers of the 14th century. Before becoming King in 1364, the Dauphin Charles's official title was Lieutenant General of the Kingdom and regent during his father's captivities. He ruled until 1380, by which time the English had been almost entirely driven from France.

Philip Duc d'Orléans was born in 1336, the fifth son of King Philip VI of France. After briefly taking part in the battle of Poitiers, he was one of the noble hostages sent to England to ensure that the terms of the Treaty of Brétigny were carried out. In 1365 King Edward III freed the Duc d'Orléans, supposedly because he had become a close friend of Edward's youngest son Thomas. He died without heirs.

Arnoul d'Audrehem was born around 1305 and first saw action against the English in Scotland in 1335. In 1342 Audrehem was appointed Captain of Brittany and was captured at Calais in 1347. After his release he was

'An Angel announces the Birth of Christ to the Shepherds in the Fields', in an English stained-glass window from the second quarter of the 14th century. Its original location is not known, but it shows the sort of peasants from whom so much of the English armies of the Hundred Years War were recruited. Some would probably have taken bagpipes with them to provide entertainment on campaign. (Victoria & Albert Museum, inv. 2270-1900, London)

made one of the King's Lieutenants in 1351 and a Marshal in 1353. He was still one of the Marshals in the French army when he was taken captive during the battle of Poitiers. He subsequently served as an ambassador for the captive King John II, being sent to raise the King's ransom. Although Audrehem continued to play a significant diplomatic role, he also fought against the English at Najera and was again captured. This resulted in a 'court of chivalry' because he had not yet paid off his ransom following capture at Poitiers. King Charles V employed Arnoul d'Audrehem as Keeper of the Gates of Paris until his death in 1370 or 1371.

John de Clermont was the son of the Lord of Thorigny. He served on campaign in Flanders and Hainault in 1340, and again in Avignon and Languedoc. Rewarded with Lordships of Boomont and Chantilly, Clermont was appointed as a Marshal of France in 1352. He was killed at the battle of Poitiers.

Gautier IV de Brienne had an extraordinary career of success and failure, inheriting the largely meaningless title of Duke of Athens and living as a refugee at the Angevin court of Naples from an early age. He married a niece of King Robert of Naples and was involved in unsuccessful campaigns to recover his Athenian inheritance. Though involved in the early campaigns of the Hundred Years War, Gautier de Brienne was offered a virtual dictatorship over Florence and Pisa in 1341. Soon forced out, he returned to France. After unsuccessful attempts to regain his position in Italy he was back in France by 1355 and was made King John's Constable, it which role he was killed at Poitiers.

OPPOSING ARMIES

There were few changes in the basic characteristics of the French and English armies during the ten years that separated the battles of Crécy and Poitiers.[5] The main elements of both remained the men-at-arms who included both knights and squires, archers who included both longbowmen and crossbowmen, and other assorted infantry. The cavalry might sometimes be regarded as 'light', but this usually reflected the fact that they and their horses were wearing less armour because of the task that had been allocated. A significant proportion of the best archers and other infantry were also mounted, though they would normally fight on foot.

This period has also been characterised as seeing 'the rise of infantry'. In spite of centuries of cavalry superiority, the basic military fact remained that horsemen remained generally ineffective against steady infantry in a defensive position. English successes in the early part of the Hundred Years War resulted from a revival of such proper trained infantry armed with longbows. However, the longbow did not itself win battles like Crécy or Poitiers. These were won because infantry archers had been effectively combined with other infantry and with men-at-arms, either on foot or on horseback.[6]

Although knights and squires came to be collectively known as men-at-arms, the status of knighthood remained significant, especially in terms of morale and leadership. Nevertheless, confusion persists where the mentality of the knightly class is concerned. Their objection to 'going on foot' like a peasant really focused on means of travel rather than fighting. The men-at-arms were also keen to preserve their horses, since these were a mark of their status as well as being very expensive.

From the mid-14th century onwards, Royal officials took ever more direct control over military supplies, resulting in a system known as *purveyance* in England or *prise* in France. Where armour and weapons were concerned there had been little change. The full plate armour of this period was very effective against close-combat weapons and against arrows, unless they were shot from close range. Consequently fully armoured men had considerable confidence in their protection. The weight of armour might be tiring over long periods, but it was well distributed and it did not limit mobility. When fighting on foot men-at-arms wore the lightest armour consistent with full protection. The main problem seems to have remained visibility and ventilation versus protection for the face.

The only part of Europe that made steel armour in the 14th century was northern Italy, from where the military elites of both England and France bought considerable amounts of such equipment by the time of Poitiers. Armour made elsewhere used various qualities of iron, normally in the form of coats-of-plates or 'brigandines'. Such armours were certainly made in France and a document from 1352 recorded that an armourer in Castelnau-de-Bressac made 60 'complete harness' for the town of Cordes.

'La Joyeuse', the so-called *Sword of Charlemagne*, which was one of the most important symbols of power and authority for the medieval French monarchy. Its pommel dates from the 9th or 10th century, the quillons from the 12th century. (Musée du Louvre, inv. MS 84, Paris)

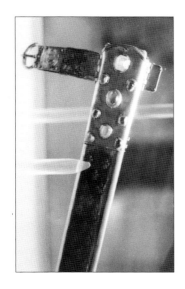

The decorated scabbard of 'La Joyeuse', the so-called *Sword of Charlemagne*, dated from the late 13th century though it was extensively restored in the 19th century. (Musée du Louvre, inv. MS 84, Paris)

The armour and weapons purchased by some towns was then sold to its citizens, often on credit. Around the time of Poitiers a version of the quilted *pourpoint* 'soft-armour' called a *jaque* came into fashion in France. It consisted of several pieces of tailored cloth with numerous buttons and a padded lining. The use of horse-armour seemingly declined during the early decades of the 14th century, despite the presence of an elite of French cavalry on armoured horses at the battle of Poitiers. Even here such armour seems to have been limited to the heads or forequarters of the animals.

ENGLISH ARMIES

The Black Prince's 'Register'[7] and the 'Day-Book' of John Henxteworth[8], who was the Prince's financial controller in Gascony, include valuable information about the 1356 campaign. Clearly the Prince was getting monies from the Exchequer as early as 26 April 1355 for the wages of men-at-arms and archers to be sent to Gascony. The Receiver-General, Peter Lacey, also paid £7,242 to knights and other men-at-arms before the expedition departed. Henry Blackburn, the receiver of the Prince's chamber, was responsible for ensuring that these men got their money and for: *all kinds of expenses made within and without the household such as gifts, alms, necessaries, messageries, wages and fees of war and other things whatsoever.* One such knight, Sir John de Lisle, died early in the expedition and a separate account shows that the expenses for himself and his retinue of 30 men-at-arms and 30 archers amounted to £343, 3s, 4d. Other fascinating details can be found in the Day-Book of John Henxteworth, which lists expenses ranging from the Black Prince's gambling debts, to the cost of repairing a ship damaged during the voyage from England and compensation for property trashed by rowdy Welsh soldiers.

Local Gascon militias had long played a major role in the defence of English possessions in south-western France, but these do not seem to have taken part in the Black Prince's expeditions of 1356. The main Gascon elements during the Prince's *chevauchées* came from the men-at-arms and local professional crossbowmen. Many of the latter probably came from poor mountain regions such as Béarn. The Black Prince's army also included *bidaus* and *brigans*, including light infantry armed with traditional javelins.

The promise of victory, booty and wealth was, of course, a significant factor in the recruitment, retention and performance of mid-14th-century armies. After the battle of Crécy soldiers returning to England spread the idea that there were easy pickings in France, a belief encouraged by King Edward III's government. Furthermore the expectation of booty often made the lowly rank-and-file willing to continue campaigning even when they had not been paid.

The size of the English army at the battle of Poitiers is a matter of debate, though the expedition that the Black Prince led from Bergerac in early August 1356 was probably smaller than he had hoped. It may initially have included between 7,000 and 10,500 men; the largest group being men-at-arms, with a slightly smaller number of archers and cross-bowmen, plus 1,000 or so other foot soldiers.

FRENCH ARMIES

French armies of the 1350s were considerably smaller than those of the early part of the Hundred Years War, though this resulted from financial rather than recruitment problems. Real improvements in discipline would, however, not be seen until after the battle of Poitiers.

Military leadership remained traditional and it was common to find bishops with substantial armed followings. For example in 1356 Guillaume de Melun, the Archbishop of Sens, led a retinue of 22 fighting men including his brother Simon de Melun plus his standard-bearer Jean de Beaulieu, and rode a warhorse worth 600 *ecus*. The Archbishop would, in fact, be taken prisoner at Poitiers.

By the 1350s the French aristocracy of *noblesse* and *chevalerie* had become a hereditary caste whose members claimed status, rank, exemption from most taxation and almost exclusive rights to the profits of war, while major provincial barons enjoyed virtual sovereignty over vast areas. There are believed to have been 40,000 to 50,000 noble families in France and consequently the French *chevalerie* formed a knightly class four times larger than that of England.

During the reign of King John II a newer system of *Semonce des Nobles* demanded service from all fief-holding nobles aged 14 to 60, those who did not serve in person having to pay money. The only other form of feudal recruitment was the *fief-rente*, which was a form of service in return for cash payment, but even this would soon go into steep decline. Instead French commanders relied on a system of verbal or written contracts to raise troops, especially men-at-arms. For example, in 1356 the recruitment of 400 *glaives* or men-at-arms was authorised for the defence of the Auvergne. French reliance on contracted *grandes compagnies* increased under John II and Charles V but it remained a rather haphazard arrangement that, unlike the English system of military contracts, rarely included a retaining fee.

The bronze effigy of Edward the Prince of Wales, popularly known as the Black Prince, provides one of the most detailed three-dimensional representations of the armour worn by the English aristocratic elite in the second half of the 14th century. Much of it would probably have been imported from northern Italy, which then manufactured the best armour in Europe. (*in situ* the Cathedral, Canterbury)

Between Crécy and Poitiers the French also recruited new types of soldiers. These included *brigans*, which had originally meant soldiers wearing light 'brigandine' armour. By the mid-14th century French *brigantes* included various sorts of infantry and the term eventually came to mean a gang of robbers. Other French troops of this period included mounted *pavesiers* or shield-bearers, and archers.

Little is known about the French crossbowmen at Poitiers although after Crécy, King Philip had decided that militia crossbowmen from the towns were 'like snow in sunshine'. His son John II apparently thought the same, and they were not apparently raised for the Poitiers campaign. France had been a peaceful country and, apart from the military aristocracy, few people had military traditions. This probably explains the continuing reliance on so-called 'Genoese' crossbowmen and infantry sergeants. Another group of low-status troops in King John II's army were the *ragacins* (from the Italian *ragazzini*), many of who came from the Alpine regions of Savoy and Italy.

King John and his Council were working on military reforms as early as 1351 when a new *Reglement pour les gens de guerre* fixed 25 as the minimum number of men-at-arms a *chevetaine* or captain could lead under his own banner. Other regulations imposed regular reviews to be held without prior warning by the Marshal's clerks. The duties of senior officers were gradually regularised and there was a new scale of military wages. In 1355 Jean d'Armagnac, the Lieutenant General in Languedoc, ordered all noblemen and troops to wear a white cross on their clothes. This contrasted with the red cross sometimes worn by English troops, though it is unclear whether either was seen at the battle of Poitiers.

Despite such attempted reform, the primary concern of the French knightly class was too often personal prestige. Their status was, of course, under threat as a result of several failures. Nevertheless, many professional soldiers were focused on the practical requirements for military success. Warfare during this period could also be very dangerous for some social groups and it has been estimated that the French aristocracy lost more men in the battles of Crécy and Poitiers than died during the Black Death.

Most French armies at the start of the Hundred Years War had included three or four times as many infantry as cavalry. This proportion declined steadily and the number of French infantry at Poitiers was relatively small. The size of King John II's army in 1356 is also a matter of conjecture. It was bigger than the Black Prince's Anglo-Gascon force, but the French King had dismissed most of his low-grade infantry before setting out in pursuit of the enemy. Some have claimed that his army numbered up to 30,000 men. A more realistic figure puts it around 8,000 cavalry, perhaps 2,000 mounted crossbowmen and maybe 1,000 or so light infantry. The highly respected French military historian Ferdinand Lot argued that the French army was actually comparable to that of the Black Prince.[9] He pointed out that the Duc d'Orléans' division reportedly included 300 fully armoured men, as did the Dauphin's division, and when the fully armoured men of the Marshals' cavalry are included this makes a total of 1,200 fully armoured men-at-arms. There may have been an equal number in the King's division, making a total of only 2,400. The Black Prince, in his letter to the Bishop of Worcester, stated that in addition to the Constable, the Duc de Bourbon and the Bishop of Châlons, 16 French *bannerets* and 2,426 men-at-arms were killed. On the other hand some French accounts claimed that only 300 were killed. Presumably the victors exaggerated and the losers reduced the total. The Friars Minor in Poitiers buried 60 knights and 42 squires. The Preaching Friars buried 18 including the Duc de Bourbon in their church and another 50 in their cloister. Prisoners in English hands, including those taken at Romorantin, supposedly numbered 1,923 men-at-arms, though this probably only referred to men worth ransoming. French sources such as the *Grandes Chroniques* say there were around 1,700 prisoners. With the known dead this comes to 2,500 men. Of the four French *batailles*, or divisions, involved at Poitiers, three were destroyed while that of the Duc d'Orléans largely escaped. Some men escaped at the end of the battle, though probably relatively few.

5 For general information about these armies see Campaign 71: *Crécy 1346 – Triumph of the Longbow*.
6 S. Morillo, 'The Age of Cavalry Revisited', in D.J. Kagay and L.J.A. Villalon (eds.), *The Circle of War in the Middle Ages* (Woodbridge, 1999) pp. 45–58.
7 In the Public Records Office in London.
8 In the Duchy of Cornwall Office.
9 F. Lot, *L'Art Militaire et les Armées au Moyen Age*, vol. 1 (Paris, 1946) p. 364.

OPPOSING PLANS

THE ENGLISH PLAN

Because Philip of Navarre, the brother of King Charles of Navarre, formed an alliance with England the newly raised English forces, which had been intended for continuing campaigning in Brittany, were redirected under the command of Duke Henry of Lancaster. In addition, Robert Knollys took 500 men-at-arms and 500 archers from the English army that was already in Brittany, while Philip of Navarre added 100 of his own Norman men-at-arms. This force, entirely mounted, set out on 22 June and a week later raised the French King's siege of Pont-Audemer. The Duke of Lancaster then moved on the vulnerable castle of Bréteuil, which was garrisoned by troops loyal to his ally, Philip of Navarre. First he resupplied Bréteuil, and then stormed the French-held towns of Conches (4 July) and Verneuil (5 July). In strategic terms these events formed the immediate background to the Black Prince's campaign in south-central France.

King John II had gathered an army to face Lancaster, but so slowly that the English evaded battle on 9 July. Two strenuous English marches then moved them beyond the reach of the French. On the other hand, Lancaster's *chevauchée* was faster moving than the Black Prince's subsequent raid and consequently unable to do so much damage. Yet it successfully resupplied important friendly castles and destroyed some enemy-held ones, while also capturing 2,000 horses. Only a few days later the Earl of Lancaster launched another *chevauchée* southwards from

A knight swearing on the Gospels in a mid- to late 14th-century French manuscript of Arthurian tales. The kneeling knight's helmet is on the floor next to him. It is a form of bascinet with a rounded or "pig-faced" visor and a mail aventail. The other knights have bascinets with their visors removed, plus close-fitting cuirasses and full armour for their arms and legs. (Bibliothèque Nationale, Ms. Fr. 343, Paris)

Brittany and this was the one that almost certainly hoped to join forces with the Black Prince, who was by then already advancing north from Bergerac.

It is even possible that King Edward III initially planned a third expedition, perhaps to be led by him personally, in northern France. This would to a large extent have repeated the English strategy seen in 1355. However, some historians maintain that Lancaster never really intended to link up with the Black Prince, and point out that the Duke had already withdrawn by the time the Prince turned south. Nevertheless the Duke of Lancaster was under contract to help the Prince if needed. Together they could have formed an army large enough to defeat the French King in battle. As the Prince's own indenture of July 1355 stated: *The king [Edward III] has promised that if it should happen that the Prince is besieged or beset by so great a force that he cannot save himself unless he be rescued by the King's power, then the King will rescue him … and the Duke of Lancaster and [a list of others] have promised and pledged their faith to give without fail all the help and counsel they can in making such a rescue.*[10]

In most respects the Poitiers campaign was like other large English *chevauchée* raids, being designed to wreak havoc and demonstrate that the French King could not defend his own people. Its purpose was to undermine loyalty to the French Crown, especially amongst the local aristocracies whose estates were being ravaged. Its primary function was not to lure the French army into a major battle; in fact, such a full-scale confrontation was to be avoided if possible. From the Black Prince's point of view the battle of Poitiers was almost certainly unwanted.

In practical terms the communications and transport problems inherent in medieval warfare meant that this sort of campaign, and French defensive moves against such raids, were largely organised locally. The English, like almost all European armies of this period, moved in the traditional three divisions of 'Vanward', 'Mainward' and 'Rearward' with their flanks protected by men-at-arms and mounted archers. The respected military historian Matthew Bennett has recently argued that the importance of superior English firepower has been greatly exaggerated.[11] Nor is Bennett convinced by the idea that the archers somehow 'funnelled' their enemies against the fully armoured English men-at-arms. Medieval English military tradition placed great emphasis on troops protecting their front by using natural or man-made obstacles. Furthermore the English were usually wary of close combat. The existing evidence also strongly suggests that English archers were normally placed on the flanks. To be fully effective such archers needed mobility, moving around and between their own protective obstacles. Consequently Bennett concludes that the primary role of archers was to protect their own men-at-arms by providing flanking fire.

Matthew Bennett has also looked at the 'herce' formation used by English archers at Poitiers and elsewhere. He points out that one

The medieval centre of Chartres, viewed from the roof of the Cathedral, which still dominates the city. Chartres often served as a mustering point for French armies during the Middle Ages, and did so in 1356 when King John II was assembling an army to march against the Black Prince. (Author's photograph)

popular interpretation of this formation, which suggests that it had 'projecting teeth', would actually have produced weak points in the English line. Furthermore archers were not well equipped to protect themselves if the enemy's armoured cavalry, or men-at-arms on foot, engaged them in close combat.

The chronicler Froissart only used the term 'herce' on three other occasions in his huge work; one being in his epic description of the battle of Poitiers. The term has usually been translated as a harrow, a large rectangular agricultural implement with protruding 'teeth' that was used to break up clods of earth. But even this meaning of the word 'herce' was extremely rare in medieval literature, so why should Froissart use it when trying to illustrate what he perhaps regarded as an unusual military formation? Other contemporary meanings for the term 'herce' or 'herse' included a sort of 'candelabrum', which would presumably have been round with spikes for the candles, and 'hedgehog', which was even more spiky. However, it is possible that all these attempted explanations have missed the point. South of the Pyrenees Mountains, in the Iberian peninsula where many of Froissart's English, French and Gascon informants had fought, there was another and more likely source for the military term 'herce'. Here, a few decades before the battle of Poitiers, a Spanish nobleman named Don Juan Manuel had included several chapters on tactics in his *Libro de los Estados*. These mentioned a formation called the *Haz* (plural *Haces*) that literally meant a 'bundle' or 'sheaf'. Although Don Manuel was writing about the cavalry warfare typical of the Iberian Peninsula, he nevertheless regarded the *Haz* as an essentially defensive formation in which the fighting men were packed closer together than usual.[12]

The attractive little town of Vierzon was sacked by the Black Prince and his Gascon allies under the Captal de Buch in the last week of August 1356. Today one of the few relics from that period is a fortified gateway known as the Beffroi or belfry. Many of the houses inside the medieval centre of Vierzon are of half-timbered construction, though it is unlikely that any of these wooden structures predate the torching of 1356. (Fred Nicolle photograph)

THE FRENCH PLAN

King John II's strategic aim was straightforward. He intended to protect the line of the river Loire and then, when the Black Prince retreated southwards, pursue the English. His intention was to overtake the Black Prince, cut his line of retreat to Gascony, and then destroy his army in battle. Almost no information survives concerning French defences facing Duke Henry of Lancaster's *chevauchée* out of Brittany and down to the Loire, but the fact that Lancaster was unable to cross the river and soon returned to the English-dominated part of Brittany suggests that they were at least adequate.

The forces that the French King John II initially sent south to the Loire, then beyond that river, were instructed to observe and harass the English. Only later did he himself advance with the main French army. The forces that preceded King John succeeded in slowing the Black Prince's progress

The front and the right side of what remains of an early to mid-14th-century iron coat-of-plates found in the castle of Küssnach in Switzerland. It is believed to date from between 1340 and 1360 and would probably have been covered in fabric when new. Such armours were the most common, though not the most up-to-date, in both the English and French armies at the battle of Poitiers. (Schweizerisches Landesmusum, inv. LM-13367, Zürich)

and, equally importantly, sent back accurate information about English numbers and English movements. Within a few days of the Black Prince turning back from Tours on the river Loire, and of the main French forces crossing that river in pursuit, King John managed to overtake his enemy.

So far things had gone entirely as King John had intended and the French had demonstrated their almost complete strategic superiority. However, it would seem that a combination of poor scouting, poor discipline and bad luck allowed the Black Prince to move south of the King's army between Chauvigny and Poitiers. The Prince subsequently claimed that he was now pursuing the French, but this was written after the English victory at the battle of Poitiers. In reality the Black Prince's relatively small raiding army was still within range of the French and it was this proximity of King John's army that obliged the Black Prince to find a strong defensible position north of the village of Nouaillé.

King John had achieved his aim of bringing the English to battle. However, the subsequent French plan of attack took into account previous painful experiences of attacking English armies in strong defensive positions, especially when the English had many archers in their ranks. The normal tradition in medieval western European and especially French warfare was for men-at-arms to attack men-at-arms. It is also clear that the French had often used flank attacks by cavalry to clear enemy archers from the field of battle. This they continued to try to do, either on horseback or on foot, in subsequent decades.

On this occasion the French commanders formed their most heavily armoured horsemen into a striking force that was intended to drive the English archers away. By dismounting almost all the rest of their men-at-arms, the French leaders hoped to make their formations – rather than the men themselves – less vulnerable to such English archers as might remain. Both these tactical decisions failed and the battle was a catastrophe for the French, with King John II himself being captured. However, these tactics did show that French armies were already trying to counter the tactical or battlefield advantages that the composition of English armies

A drawings of the now lost carved stone effigy of Pierre Millet, the Seigneur du Plessis. This effigy dated from the mid-14th century and shows typical armour of the French military elite of this period. The drawing was made by Roger de Gaignières in the 17th century. (Bibliothèque Nationale, Res. Pe. 11a, fol., Paris)

gave to English commanders. As such, although unsuccessful, it was a first step in a long but ultimately victorious struggle.

Where the battle of Poitiers itself was concerned, the conventions of the period meant that a full-scale formal confrontation was regarded as a matter of mutual consent by the two armies, following formal challenges. For this both sides were supposed to be ready and prepared. In fact the famous French knight Geoffroi de Charny, who was killed while carrying the sacred Oriflamme banner at Poitiers, wrote in his treatise on knighthood that anyone who attacked another without a proper defiance or challenge was not worthy to be called a man-at-arms. Given the fact that other forms of warfare, such as ambush and even the raiding that the English had been doing so far, had considerably lower prestige among the knightly aristocracy, many in both armies probably welcomed the opportunity for a formal battle. Such traditional attitudes would be clearly seen amongst the elite of the losing side who were very concerned to avoid surrendering to an enemy of low status.

10 H.J. Hewitt, *The Black Prince's Expedition of 1355–1357* (Manchester, 1958) p. 106.
11 M. Bennett, 'The Development of Battle Tactics in the Hundred Years War', in A. Curry & M. Hughes (eds.), *Arms, Armies and Fortifications in the Hundred Years War* (Woodbridge, 1994) pp. 1–22.
12 J.M. Castro y Calvo (ed.), *El arte de gobernar en las obras de Don Juan Manuel* (Barcelona, 1945); translated extracts in D. Nicolle, 'Medieval Warfare: The Unfriendly Interface', *Journal of Military History*, 63 (July 1999) p. 598–9.

THE CAMPAIGN

The Black Prince assembled his English forces at Bergerac on the river Dordogne. Here they were joined by most of the local Gascon contingents. Not all would accompany the Prince on his *chevauchée* into the centre of France, however. In fact a substantial force was separated from the main army to protect English-ruled Gascony while the Black Prince was away. These troops were left under the command of the *Seneschal* John de Chiverston, Bernard d'Albret and the Mayor of Bordeaux.

THE BLACK PRINCE'S *CHEVAUCHÉE*

On 4 August 1356 the Black Prince and the rest of his troops left Bergerac and marched through fertile countryside to Périgueux, which had been captured by pro-English forces a few months before. The Prince himself spent the night of 6 August outside the city at the Château l'Evêque, which was the summer residence of the Bishops of Périgueux. The following night they were at Ramefort. Leaving the valley of the river Isle two days later, they entered the valley of the Dronne at Brantôme and spent the night in and around the Abbey where, however, there was no record of any damage being inflicted.

The Anglo-Gascon army then advanced to Quisser (10 August) where the castle was too strong to assault. At Nontron (11 August) they reportedly found large supplies of fish. The raiders were now in the Limousin region where they inflicted as much damage at they could. Passing through Rochechouart (12 August) to the Benedictine Priory of La Péruse near Confolens (13 August), where the Prince spent the night, they reached Lesterps on 14 August. Here the canons of the church of St Pierre defied their assault for a day but eventually had to give in. In response the Prince spared the monks, townspeople and church, supposedly out of admiration for their courage.

By now the invaders had covered over 150 kilometres (93 miles) in ten days. Two days later they reached Bellac, where they rested for two days and did no damage because the place belonged to the widow of the Earl of Pembroke who was thus related to the English Royal family. According to Froissart: *The Prince of Wales and his army ... rode forward at their ease and gathered provisions of all kinds in great profusion, being astonished to find the province of Auvergne ... so rich and well provisioned ... They burned and pillaged the whole land, when they entered into a town and found it richly stocked with food they refreshed themselves for two or three days and then departed, destroyed what remained, smashing barrels of wine and burning fields of wheat and oats.*

Apart from a few minor skirmishes, the raiders had met very little resistance so far. Nevertheless, according to Geoffrey le Baker, the Prince

A restored version of the damaged portrait of King John II, called The Good, attributed to Girart d'Orléans. The original shows the French King shortly after he came to the throne in 1350. (Musée du Louvre, Paris)

OPERATIONS IN FRANCE, JANUARY TO 28 AUGUST 1356

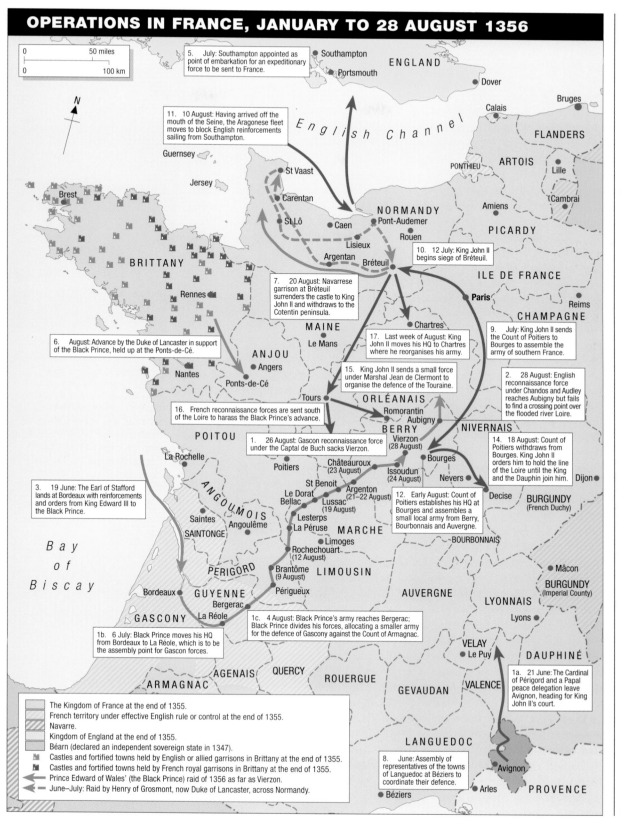

0   50 miles
0   100 km

5.   July: Southampton appointed as point of embarkation for an expeditionary force to be sent to France.

11.   10 August: Having arrived off the mouth of the Seine, the Aragonese fleet moves to block English reinforcements sailing from Southampton.

10.   12 July: King John II begins siege of Bréteuil.

7.   20 August: Navarrese garrison at Bréteuil surrenders the castle to King John II and withdraws to the Cotentin peninsula.

6.   August: Advance by the Duke of Lancaster in support of the Black Prince, held up at the Ponts-de-Cé.

17.   Last week of August: King John II moves his HQ to Chartres where he reorganises his army.

9.   July: King John II sends the Count of Poitiers to Bourges to assemble the army of southern France.

15.   King John II sends a small force under Marshal Jean de Clermont to organise the defence of the Touraine.

2.   28 August: English reconnaissance force under Chandos and Audley reaches Aubigny but fails to find a crossing point over the flooded river Loire.

16.   French reconnaissance forces are sent south of the Loire to harass the Black Prince's advance.

1.   26 August: Gascon reconnaissance force under the Captal de Buch sacks Vierzon.

14.   18 August: Count of Poitiers withdraws from Bourges. King John II orders him to hold the line of the Loire until the King and the Dauphin join him.

3.   19 June: The Earl of Stafford lands at Bordeaux with reinforcements and orders from King Edward III to the Black Prince.

12.   Early August: Count of Poitiers establishes his HQ at Bourges and assembles a small local army from Berry, Bourbonnais and Auvergne.

1b.   6 July: Black Prince moves his HQ from Bordeaux to La Réole, which is to be the assembly point for Gascon forces.

1c.   4 August: Black Prince's army reaches Bergerac; Black Prince divides his forces, allocating a smaller army for the defence of Gascony against the Count of Armagnac.

1a.   21 June: The Cardinal of Périgord and a Papal peace delegation leave Avignon, heading for King John II's court.

8.   June: Assembly of representatives of the towns of Languedoc at Béziers to coordinate their defence.

The Kingdom of France at the end of 1355.
French territory under effective English rule or control at the end of 1355.
Navarre.
Kingdom of England at the end of 1355.
Béarn (declared an independent sovereign state in 1347).
Castles and fortified towns held by English or allied garrisons in Brittany at the end of 1355.
Castles and fortified towns held by French royal garrisons in Brittany at the end of 1355.
Prince Edward of Wales' (the Black Prince) raid of 1356 as far as Vierzon.
June–July: Raid by Henry of Grosmont, now Duke of Lancaster, across Normandy.

31

placed two experienced commanders, John Chandos and James Audley, in charge of his scouts during his march through the regions of Limousin and Berry. Meanwhile: *He himself took charge of the camp, seeing that it was moved each day when the road had been inspected, and provided with defences against night attacks. He also saw that the usual watch was kept, and went around them himself with his more valiant comrades, each part of the army being visited in case something out of the ordinary exposed it to danger.*[13]

After leaving Bellac the Prince's advance became more difficult. In the region of Berry the locals fought back, though not very effectively. Le Dorat with its great fortified church fell first, then the town of Lussac les Eglises (19 August) where some years later Sir John Chandos would be killed. The Anglo-Gascons then passed through Saint Benoit de Sault (20 August) to Argenton (21–22 August) where the castle was taken. Although the raiders ranged over a wide area they generally spared churches and the property of friends. They passed by the city of Châteauroux (23 August), which they did not take.

The famous Château of Saumur dominates the Loire about 45 kilometres (28 miles) upriver from Angers. Part of the castle dates from the 13th century but most was built in the later 14th century, after some of King John II's army had crossed the Loire at this point in pursuit of the Black Prince. (Author's photograph)

Here the Black Prince wrote that he intended going to Bourges where he expected to find the Count of Poitiers. The following day was the feast of St Bartholomew, so the Anglo-Gascon army rested. In fact the Black Prince did not himself go to Bourges. An English raiding party burned its suburbs but were unable to take the fortified *cité*, which was defended by the archbishop and two senior knights sent by King John. According to Froissart; *At one of the gates there was a heavy skirmish, involving the two knights from within the city, the Seigneur de Gonsant and Sir Hutin de Vermeilles and many gallent [sic] deeds were performed in that action.* The main Anglo-Gascon army reached Issoudun on 24 August but, despite a full-scale assault, was again unable to take the fortified *cité*, defended by local noblemen and their followers. On the 26th the Black Prince moved on, after burning Issoudun's suburbs.

During 28 August the Black Prince's army marched along the small rivers Théols and Arnon, took the castle of La Ferté, left the Arnon at Lury, which stood on the ancient boundary of the Duchy of Guyenne, and crossed the river Cher. It was probably also on 28 August that an Anglo-Gascon raiding party of 200 troops under Chandos and Audley, on its way back to the Black Prince having seized Aubigny-sur-Nère only 25 kilometres (16 miles) from the river Loire, bumped into a French reconnaissance force. The French were commanded by Philip de Chambly, nicknamed Grismouton, whose orders were to send King John II reports on the location and activities of the invaders. Since the English also took some prisoners in this skirmish, the Black Prince learned that the French King had mustered a large army and was determined to meet him in battle. John II was then at Chartres, though he hoped to meet the English near Orléans on their way towards Tours. Orléans was to have been the next English target but the Prince, having cross the river Cher, now turned aside and travelled west towards Vierzon. The speed of the raiders' progress had also now slowed.

A woman cooking over an open fire, in a collection of Roman laws by the 12th-century Italian monk Gratian. This mid-14th-century copy included a commentary by Barthélemy of Brescia and its illustrations show aspects of everyday and camp life. The scene shown here could have been found in both the French and English camps. (*Concordia Discordantium Canonum*, Bibliothèque Municipale, Ms. 5128, f. 91, Lyon)

Froissart described Vierzon as 'a large town with a strong castle, but poorly fortified and lightly garrisoned.' It had, in fact, already fallen to the Gascon advance guard under the Captal de Buch on 26 August, its garrison being too small to resist the approaching enemy. The population fled and the Gascons looted any supplies they could find. Two days later the main English army arrived, stayed three days then burned the town and moved on. It was at Vierzon that, according to Froissart: *News reached the Prince of Wales that the King of France was at Chartres, and that all the towns on the Loire and all means of crossing the river were so well guarded that he would find no way of getting north of it. The prince therefore took counsel and descided [sic] to beat a retreat, through Touraine and Poitou, skirmishing as he went and burning and pillaging the country.*[14]

Meanwhile another English army led by the Duke of Lancaster had reached the Loire. There Lancaster found the bridges either broken or heavily defended. His army tried to force a crossing at Les Ponts-de-Cé south of Angers, but was baulked by a large island fortress that guarded the northern channel. Since the Loire was flooded and could only be crossed by bridge, and there were no other bridges between Nantes and Saumur, both of which had strong walls and large garrisons, there was little that Lancaster could do.

King John's army had been tied up for a month, besieging Bréteuil in Normandy without success. Royal prestige did not permit failure but John II had to bring this siege to an end so that he could face a greater danger looming in the south. An honourable compromise was reached whereby King John paid the pro-Navarrese garrison to abandon the castle. They were also allowed free passage to rejoin Philip of Navarre in western Normandy.

KING JOHN GATHERS THE FRENCH ARMY

According to Froissart, King John II now returned to Paris and ordered his nobles to gather at Chartres. The King himself arrived with a large armed retinue on 28 August. There he remained during early September, gathering intelligence about Anglo-Gascon movements. Meanwhile French troops assembled from the regions of Auvergne, Berry, Burgundy, Lorraine, Hainault, Artois, Vermandois, Picardy, Brittany and Normandy. They were to serve the King without payment for 40 days, after which they would be paid. Those unable to attend were supposed to send money with which to hire mercenaries. As these men arrived they rode past in review before being lodged in the vicinity, accommodation being arranged by the Marshals Jean de Clermont and Arnoul d'Audrehem. However, the King dismissed much of his infantry so that the army could move fast and catch the Black Prince.

One of the King's first actions was to send reinforcements to the main fortresses in Anjou, Poitou, Maine, Touraine and other areas where the invaders might appear. Their role was to stop the enemy gathering food

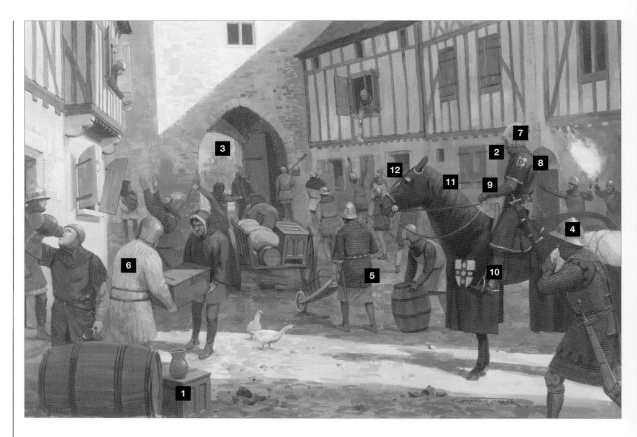

THE LOOTING OF VIERZON (pages 34–35)

On 26 August 1356 a large reconnaissance force of Gascon troops, commanded by Jean de Grailly, the Captal de Buch, seized the fortified town of Vierzon. The garrison defending this place had been too small to resist the approaching Anglo-Gascon enemy and so abandoned the town, after which the population also fled. The capture, looting and destruction of towns like Vierzon formed an essential part of medieval western European military strategy, and such *chevauchées* were brought to a fine art by the English and their allies during the Hundred Years War. This strategy was, in fact, a form of economic warfare designed to undermine an enemy's will and capability to fight. They were also intended to convince the local population, and the local aristocratic leadership, that their current ruler – in this case the King of France – was unable to defend them and thus no longer deserved their support. The so-called 'feudal' structure of society was, after all, a form of social contract in which rulers were expected to provide protection in return for loyalty. Two days later the main English army under the Black Prince reached Vierzon. They stayed outside its fortifications for three days, helping the Captal de Buch and his Gascons collect any supplies they could find. This included considerable quantities of food and wine (1). The Anglo-Gascon soldiers then burned the town before moving on. In this illustration the Captal de Buch (2) supervises looting and destruction around one of Vierzon's fortified gates (3), which survives, little changed, to this day. All sorts of troops took part in *chevauchées*, though most of the destruction seems to have been carried out by specially designated 'ravagers' who would probably have been more lightly equipped than usual so that they could range far afield and move at high speed. Here the Captal's Gascon troops largely consisted of fully armoured men-at-arms (4), armoured foot soldiers (5) and the light infantry (6) who were typical of the mountainous Pyrenean regions of southern France. Jean de Grailly, the Captal de Buch, is himself shown wearing a fine quality steel bascinet (7); a form of helmet that included a pivot for a removable visor. Its mail aventail stands proud of his chin and shoulders since there is a thick layer of padding beneath. The Captal de Buch's surcoat (8) is similarly padded and has his coat-of-arms – a black cross on a gold ground with white scallop shells – on thickly embroidered panels sewn to its sleeves and chest. His armour consists of a long-sleeved mail hauberk with integral gloves (9), and iron greaves (10) on the fronts of his legs only. These are worn over mail chausses. Jean de Grailly's coat-of-arms is repeated in his horse's cloth caparison (11). The only visible horse-armour is a hardened leather panel (12) riveted to the exterior of this caparison, over the horse's head, and there is another larger hardened leather panel on the inside just visible around the horse's eyes. One of the problems inherent in *chevauchée* warfare was that the raiding force could easily become over-burdened with loot that slowed it down and made it vulnerable to interception. It took a particularly effective and respected leader to convince common soldiers, often from poor backgrounds, to abandon what was probably the greatest wealth that had ever passed through their hands! (Graham Turner)

and fodder. As Froissart put it, the King of France also: *sent three important noblemen, good warriors, into the province of Berry, to guard its boundaries and discover the whereabouts of the English troops. These were the Sire de Craon, Boucicault and the Hermite de Chaumont.*

After leaving Chartres the King and his almost entirely mounted army headed for the river Loire, reaching Meung on 8 September and Blois two days later. They crossed at several points, John himself at Blois, before marching to Amboise. By the 13th the King had reached Loches where his units assembled to prepare for the chase. A steady stream of reports confirmed that the Anglo-Gascons were in the Touraine area but were now heading back towards Poitou. So King John left Loches and reached La Haye on 14 September while other contingents crossed the Loire bridges at Orléans, Meung, Saumur, Blois, Tours and perhaps elsewhere.

For a long time the war between France and England had been a great concern to the Pope in Avignon, who considered that two of Christendom's mightiest powers should join forces to take the Holy Land from the Muslims rather than fight each other. So, as Froissart recorded: *The holy father Pope Innocent VI sent to France Talleyrand, Cardinal of Périgord, and Nicholas, Cardinal of Urgel, to treat for peace … They had several times visited and spoken with the King during the siege of Bréteuil but without achieving any results … The Cardinal of Périgord went to the fair city of Tours in Touraine where news reached him that the King of France was making all speed to find the English.* So the Cardinal of Périgord hurried to Poitiers where he correctly expected the rival armies to meet.

The village known as La Haye in the Middle Ages is now called Descartes, in honour of the famous French philosopher René Descartes, who spent most of his childhood in the nearby town of Châtellerault. The ancient name is preserved only in that of a simple medieval church, Notre Dame de la Haye, which stands next to the deep-flowing river Creuse. The Black Prince and King John II crossed the Creuse at this point on 13 and 14 September 1356 respectively. (Author's photograph)

The capture of Romorantin

Meanwhile the Sire de Craon, Boucicault, the Hermite de Chaumont and their 300 or so 'lances' (men-at-arms plus retainers) had been closely observing the invaders for six days before they found an opportunity to engage their vanguard. Froissart maintained that this was because the English planned their marches and camps with such skill. However, the small French force believed they had a chance some way upriver from Romorantin. There they ambushed Bartholomew de Burghersh, Edward Despencer and Lord Essex. Froissart once again provides a vivid description: *Some troops were ordered off at once towards Romorantin, who, hearing that the English were to pass that way, lay quietly in ambush at a short distance from the town to surprise them. After a time the English came up and were suffered by the French to pass the defile without molestation, but the moment they were clear of it the French mounted their horse, and at full speed rode forward to overtake them. The English, hearing the sound of horses' feet, turned, and finding it was the enemy, immediately halted to wait for them, and the French advanced at the gallop, with their lances in their rests. So great, indeed, was their speed, that as soon as they came up the English opened their ranks, and the French were carried through on their horses without much damage. The English troops then closed, and attacked the French rear. A sharp engagement ensued, many knights and squires*

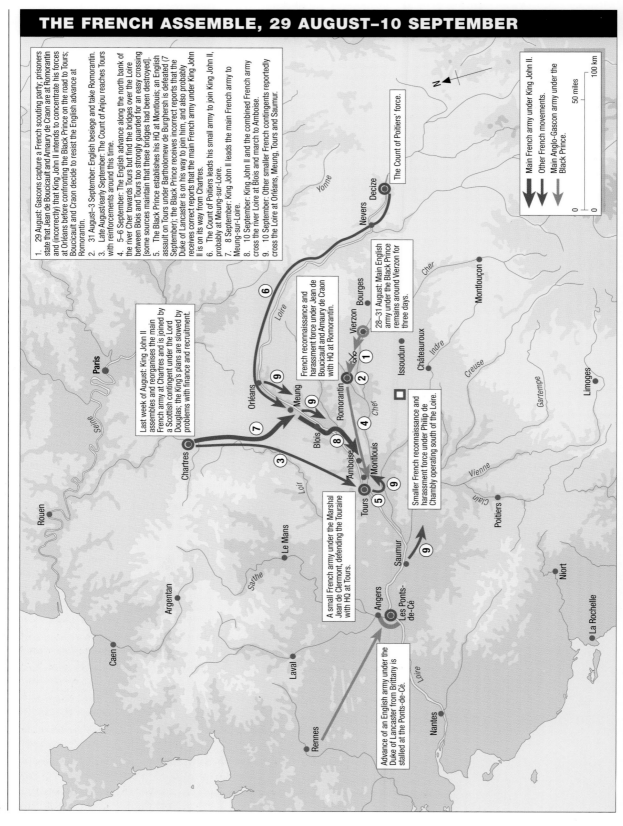

1. 29 August: Gascons capture a French scouting party; prisoners state that Jean de Boucicault and Amaury de Craon are at Romorantin and (incorrectly) that King John II intends to concentrate his forces at Orléans before confronting the Black Prince on the road to Tours; Boucicault and Craon decide to resist the English advance at Romorantin.

2. 31 August–3 September: English besiege and take Romorantin.

3. Late August/early September: The Count of Anjou reaches Tours with reinforcements around this time.

4. 5–6 September: The English advance along the north bank of the river Cher towards Tours but find the bridges over the Loire between Blois and Tours too strongly guarded for an easy crossing [some sources maintain that these bridges had been destroyed].

5. The Black Prince establishes his HQ at Montlouis; an English assault on Tours under Bartholomew de Burghersh is defeated (7 September); the Black Prince receives incorrect reports that the Duke of Lancaster is on his way to join him, and also probably receives correct reports that the main French army under King John II is on its way from Chartres.

6. The Count of Poitiers leads his small army to join King John II, probably at Meung-sur-Loire.

7. 8 September: King John II leads the main French army to Meung-sur-Loire.

8. 10 September: King John II and the combined French army cross the river Loire at Blois and march to Amboise.

9. 10 September: Other smaller French contingents reportedly cross the Loire at Orléans, Meung, Tours and Saumur.

The Count of Poitiers' force.

Main French army under King John II.

Other French movements.

Main Anglo-Gascon army under the Black Prince.

0   50 miles

0   100 km

28–31 August: Main English army under the Black Prince remains around Vierzon for three days.

French reconnaissance and harassment force under Jean de Boucicault and Amaury de Craon with HQ at Romorantin.

Last week of August: King John II assembles and reorganises the main French army at Chartres and is joined by a Scottish contingent under the Lord Douglas; the King's plans are slowed by problems with finance and recruitment.

A small French army under the Marshal Jean de Clermont, defending the Touraine with HQ at Tours.

Smaller French reconnaissance and harassment force under Philip de Chambly operating south of the Loire.

Advance of an English army under the Duke of Lancaster from Brittany is stalled at the Ponts-de-Cé.

Paris

Rouen

Chartres

Orléans

Meung

Blois

Amboise

Montlouis

Tours

Romorantin

Vierzon

Bourges

Issoudun

Châteauroux

Montluçon

Nevers

Decize

Limoges

Poitiers

Saumur

Angers

Les Ponts-de-Cé

Le Mans

Laval

Nantes

Rennes

Caen

Argentan

Niort

La Rochelle

Seine

Loir

Sarthe

Cher

Cher

Loire

Loire

Yonne

Indre

Creuse

Gartempe

Vienne

Clain

A wounded knight is carried to a monastery after a battle, in a mid- to late 14th century French manuscript of Arthurian tales. Both men have sabatons, a form of laminated armour over their feet, and these follow the fashion for very long toes current in civilian costume that would have been extremely impractical when fighting on foot. (Bibliothèque Nationale, Ms. Fr. 343, Paris)

were unhorsed on both sides, and many killed.[15] When the rest of the English vanguard arrived the French retreated, half of them escaping to the castle of Romorantin.

The Prince's decision to attack Romorantin is normally seen as a mistake because he knew that the French King was marching against him with a substantial army. Delaying the Black Prince may, of course, have been the intention of the handful of French troops who now defied him and the resulting siege lasted five days before the castle was forced to surrender. Worse still, English supplies were seriously depleted by this siege.

The assault on Romorantin castle was described by both Froissart and Geoffrey le Baker. According to Froissart: *On the next morning all the men-at-arms and archers prepared for battle, and each reporting to his own livery troop they made a sudden assault on the castle of Romorantin. The attack was fierce and heavy; the* [English] *archers who had been posted on the counterscarp sent such a continuous rain of arrows that scarcely anyone dared to show himself on the battlements. Some entered into the water up to their necks and came to the walls. Others took to the moat, floating on gates and wattles, with pikes and pickaxes, bows and arrows in their hands, to hew and pick at the base of the walls. Up above them the Seigneur de Craon, Boucicault and the Hermite de Chaumont were eagerly carrying out the task of defence, throwing down rocks and stones and pots full of quicklime.* The Captal de Buch and his Gascons were involved in this attack, a squire named Raymond de Zedulach being killed.

Next day the attack was resumed even more fiercely and again one of the most senior casualties on the English side was a Gascon, the brother of the Lord d'Albret. The Prince now declared openly that he would not

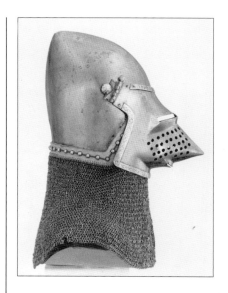

Side and rear views of an exceptionally fine-quality late 14th-century Italian bascinet helmet with a so-called dog-faced visor and a mail aventail fastened beneath vervelles and a strip of soft leather. Though made a generation or so after the battle of Poitiers, it is the same as the most up-to-date armour worn by the elites on both sides in that struggle. (Royal Armouries, Leeds)

move on until Romorantin fell. Le Baker described how the keep was finally taken: *The prince gave orders that stone-throwing machines and tortoises for protection for the miners should be built. The machines, manned by specially trained troops, destroyed the roof of the tower* [the central keep of the castle] *and the battlements with round stones. They also set fire to the* [props supporting the] *tunnel which the miners had dug and which reached to the foundations of the castle.*[16] According to Froissart the roof of the tower was also set on fire, perhaps by cannon though this is by no means clear.

After taking Romorantin, the Black Prince continued west along the Cher, apparently still hoping to join forces with the Duke of Lancaster. He made camp at Montlouis near Tours while sending out raiders and scouts. Tours itself was under the nominal command of two of the French King's sons, the Counts of Poitiers and Anjou, supported by the Marshal Clermont. Le Baker reported that heavy rain storms frustrated an English assault and: *Thanks to St Martin, the patron saint of Tours, its enemies were unable to burn the town.*

After four days waiting for Lancaster it became obvious that the Black Prince must retreat. As he stated in a letter addressed to the citizens of London after the campaign was over: *Upon our departure from thence, we took the road so as to pass certain dangers by water, and with the intention of meeting with our most dear cousin, the Duke of Lancaster, of whom we had certain news that he would make haste to draw towards us.*[17] Though the Duke of Lancaster's army could not cross the Loire, the two commanders were clearly in contact via messengers.

THE PURSUIT OF THE BLACK PRINCE

King John II's pursuit of the Black Prince now began in earnest. On 11 September the Prince turned south, crossed the Cher and the Indre and arrived at Montbazon that same evening. He knew that the French were chasing him and had the bridge over the Cher destroyed. Surrounding villages were also burned to prevent the enemy finding shelter or food. Next morning, at Montbazon, the Cardinal of Périgord arrived, urging the Prince to make peace, but the Prince replied only his father had the authority to do that. In reality King Edward had given the Black Prince authority to negotiate in a letter dated August 1356. Despite this gesture of defiance, Prince Edward continued his retreat, reaching La Haye (modern Descartes) on 13 September. There his scouts brought news that the French army was very close behind. Early next morning the Prince left La Haye, crossed the Creuse and headed for Châtellerault.

King John left Loches the same morning and after receiving information from his scouts headed for La Haye where he heard that the Prince was heading for Châtellerault. Some sources suggest that the English army's baggage train took a long time to cross the Vienne at Châtellerault; others that the baggage crossed the day before the main army, which crossed the river during the morning of Saturday 17 September.

The net begins to close

King John II decided that, instead of following in the Prince's footsteps, he would try to overtake him by remaining east of the Vienne then crossing at Chauvigny. This clever and successful manoeuvre was probably based upon superior local knowledge. Meanwhile the Prince hesitated at Châtellerault, seeking information about the French. Apparently he did not realise how close they were, or perhaps the local people misled his scouts.

On 16 September the Black Prince suddenly learned that King John was at Chauvigny and that he had been overtaken. Unless he was prepared to face the French in battle in a place of their choosing, the Prince had no choice except a rapid retreat. So far the main Anglo-Gascon force had used main roads but at dawn on Saturday morning they left the old Roman road (now the N 10) along the west bank of the Clain and veered left with the intention of rejoining the main road south of Poitiers. This might seem an obvious move for a modern army but it was a daring gamble for a medieval commander, and King John II failed to anticipate it.

Both armies were sending out scouts and foragers so it is surprising that the King failed to learn that the Prince was heading into the forest. In contrast, around Friday 17 September, the Prince judged that the French were not far off: *On his side the Prince of Wales and his men knew nothing of the disposition of the French forces, nor could they, for though they knew they were on the march they did not know exactly where, but merely that they could not be far off, for their scouts found great difficulty in producing forage* [sic], *with the result that the army suffered a serious lack of provisions.*[18]

Because it took medieval armies so long to cross rivers, even by bridges, the Prince probably hoped to surprise the French while they were divided on both sides of the Vienne. But he was too slow and, reaching the Chauvigny to Poitiers road, his scouts found that the French main force had already passed. Now the Black Prince decided to shadow them along country tracks and forest paths south of the main road. Though difficult, this largely hid the Anglo-Gascon army from French scouts.

King John had actually reached Chauvigny on the evening of Thursday 15 September. According to Froissart: *After breakfast on Friday the King of France crossed the river by the bridge at Chauvigny, thinking that the*

A drawing of the now lost carved stone effigy of Peter I, the Duc de Bourbon, who was killed at the battle of Poitiers. It used to be in the Church of the Jacobins in Paris but was destroyed during the French Revolution. The drawing was made by Roger de Gaignières in the 17th century. (Bibliothèque Nationale, Rés. Pe 1, fol. 29 & B. 7140)

THE FRENCH PURSUIT, 11–18 SEPTEMBER

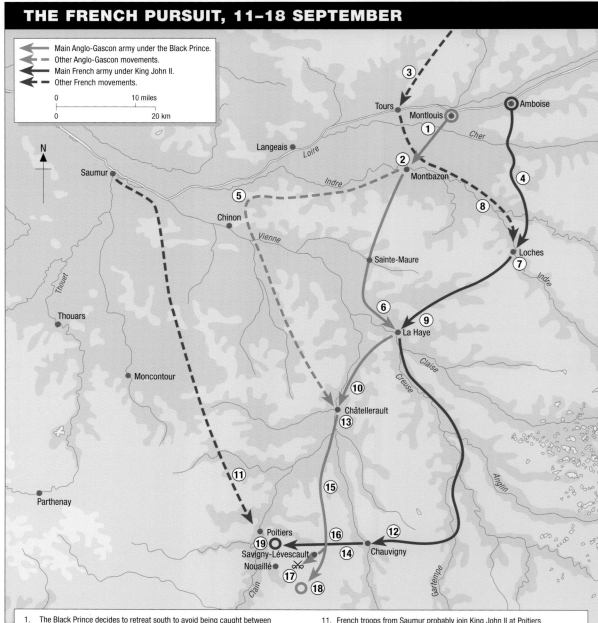

Main Anglo-Gascon army under the Black Prince.
Other Anglo-Gascon movements.
Main French army under King John II.
Other French movements.

0 ___ 10 miles
0 ___ 20 km

1. The Black Prince decides to retreat south to avoid being caught between French forces in Tours and Amboise; crosses the rivers Cher and Indre, reaching Montbazon (September 11).
2. 12 September: The Cardinal of Périgord and his retinue meet the Black Prince in an unsuccessful effort to negotiate peace.
3. 12 September (approx): French forces from Chartres under the Dauphin Charles probably reach Tours around this date.
4. French forces under King John II march along the 'Royal Road' from Amboise towards Poitiers.
5. 13 September: The Black Prince sends scouts to the west in the hope of finding the army of the Duke of Lancaster.
6. 13 September: The Black Prince's own army reaches La Haye (modern Descartes) on the river Creuse.
8. 4 September: The Dauphin Charles and his troops probably join King John II at Loches.
9. 14 September: King John II reaches La Haye.
10. 14 September: The Black Prince reaches Châtellerault on the river Vienne and remains there three days in the hope of making contact with the army of the Duke of Lancaster.

11. French troops from Saumur probably join King John II at Poitiers.
12. 15 September: King John II reaches Chauvigny.
13. 16 September: The Black Prince decides to face King John II in battle, hoping to attack the French as they are crossing the Vienne at Chauvigny.
14. 17 September: King John II and the French army march westward from Chauvigny towards Poitiers, crossing in front of the English line of march.
15. 17 September: The English leave Châtellerault and head south, marching through forests between the Clain and Vienne rivers.
16. 17 September: When they reach the road from Chauvigny to Poitiers the English find that the French have already passed and are heading for Poitiers; the English continue south into the forest.
17. 17 September: Gascon troops of the Captal de Buch attack part of the French rearguard at La Chaboterie, between Savigny-Levescault and Nouaillé, capturing the Count of Auxerre, the Count of Joigny and Jean de Châtillon. The French rearguard moves northward along the Roman road between Limoges and Poitiers.
18. 17 September: English withdraw into the forest and make camp.
19. 18 September: The French army draws up in battle array between Poitiers and Savigny-Levescault.

42

The river Vienne at Châtellerault formed a significant barrier to an army in the mid-14th century. The town also marked the normal upper limit of commercial navigation on the Vienne. The Black Prince remained here for three days, hoping for news of the Duke of Lancaster's supporting army. (Author's photograph)

English were ahead of him while in fact they were behind. Apparently the bulk of the French cavalry crossed the Vienne at Chauvigny while other troops, perhaps infantry, supposedly crossed at Châtellerault. This could suggest that the King and his men-at-arms had pressed ahead in their effort to overtake the invaders, or perhaps local infantry had joined the army since it crossed the Loire.

Three senior French lords, the Seigneur de Craon, Raoul de Coucy and the Comte de Joigny, remained in Chauvigny for a while with some of their troops. Then, on Saturday morning, they crossed the river and followed about 15 kilometres (9 miles) behind the main army. Whereas the King went along the main road from Chauvigny to Poitiers, this detached rearguard marched along agricultural tracks beside a wood south of the main road. Were they, in fact, aware that the Black Prince was now similarly south of the Chauvigny to Poitiers road?

For his part it is unlikely that the Prince was trying to catch the French and force a battle when their outriders bumped into each other at the manor of La Chaboterie, as he later claimed. What seems to have happened is that, on the evening the three French lords left Chauvigny, the Anglo-Gascon army left the village where they had rested. Gascon scouts went to find the French and Froissart as usual provides the most colourful account: *These scouts numbered about sixty men-at-arms, all well mounted according to their condition, though their horses were somewhat tired. Among them were two knights from Hainault, Sir Eustace d'Aubrecicourt and Sir Jean de Ghistelles, and they found themselves by chance near to those woods and heaths …* [through which the French were passing] *The French barons and their men … as soon as they saw the English horses, knew at once that it was the enemy and immediately put on their helmets, unfurled their banners, lowered their lances, and put spurs to their horses. Sir Eustace d'Aubrecicourt and his companions, who were mounted on the finest chargers, saw coming towards them so great a force of the enemy, and they a mere handful of men by comparison, that they thought it best not to stand, but allowed themselves to be pursued, for the Prince and his army were not far off. They therefore turned their horses about and took to the edge of the forest with the French after them … Thus riding hard in pursuit they got so far forward that they came upon the Prince's army where it had halted alongside a wood, among the heather and the brambles, waiting for news of their fellows. There was great astonishment when they saw them thus pursued.*[19] As a result most of this French band were killed or captured. Those taken included Raoul de Coucy, the Comte de Joigny, the Vicomte de Breuse, and the Seigneur de Chauvigny, from whom the Black Prince learned the location of the main French army.

According to Le Baker, the Black Prince's forces lost many killed in this skirmish. Others pursued the remaining French toward the village of Savigny-Lévescault, which disrupted the Anglo-Gascon line of march. Eventually the English and Gascons withdrew into the forest to regroup. The Black Prince gave orders that, on pain of death, none should move

ahead of the English Marshals. They camped for the night and searched vainly for water, probably in the woods of Breuil l'Abbaye close to the farm of La Chaboterie where King John II had spent the previous night. Meanwhile the main French army camped in 'battle formation' between Poitiers and Savigny-Lévescault where the bishops of Poitiers had their country residence. They were probably close to the ancient Roman road and may have selected this position before knowing exactly where the English were.

It would seem that the Anglo-Gascon army was now so close to the French, and so low on supplies, that it dared not attempt outrunning its enemies. A major confrontation was apparently inevitable and poor scouting had placed the Black Prince in a far worse tactical situation than his father had faced at Crécy. On the other hand his commanders got their men into a very good defensive position on the edge of the forest of Nouaillé.

The resulting battle of Poitiers, or of Maupertius as it is normally known in France, is one of the best-known medieval battles. However, there is still debate about its exact location. Maupertius, which meant 'bad road', is today generally assumed to have been a farmstead where the modern farm of La Cardinerie now stands. However, it seems more likely that the original 'bad road' was the track – now a minor road – from La Cardinerie to the Gué de l'Homme ford (now a bridge) across the river Miosson west of Nouaillé village.

THE EVE OF BATTLE

At sunrise on the morning of Sunday 18 September, the Black Prince's army broke camp and moved down the valley of the Miosson, apparently without French scouts noticing. Using a small country track they passed the Abbey at Nouaillé as if heading for the Poitiers to Bordeaux road. Some foragers apparently crossed the Miosson to obtain food supplies from the Abbey at Nouaillé where there was a simple bridge or a causeway forming a stabilised ford. Although none of the sources mention French scouts at Nouaillé, it seems incredible that they should not have been stationed there. If such observers were present, then perhaps they believed that the Black Prince intended following the Miosson until it joined the river Clain at Saint Benoit. The Captal de Buch's reconnaissance cavalry had been ahead of the Anglo-Gascon column and shortly after dawn they

The massive Château of Touffou dominated the valley of the Vienne north of Chauvigny. Its central keep dates from the 12th century while the outer wall and towers mostly date from the 14th. It was just this sort of powerful fortification that *chévauchée* raids like that of the Black Prince could rarely take. In fact, in 1356 the retreating Anglo-Gascon raiders avoided the valley altogether and made their way through the forested hills behind. (Author's photograph)

found the main French camp some distance north of Nouaillé wood. This suggests that the Captal's men were ranging north of the Miosson stream, which would have made sense under the circumstances; or perhaps it was they who crossed the Miosson at Nouaillé.

The vanguard of the Black Prince's army was commanded by the Earls of Warwick and Oxford, probably with the Lord of Pommiers, several other Gascon barons and the Gascon light infantry. The Prince commanded the centre, followed by the rearguard under Salisbury and probably Suffolk. As normal, their baggage brought up the rear. Again apparently unnoticed by the French, the Anglo-Gascon army then abruptly turned north, almost certainly across the Gué de l'Homme ford. Warwick, who had been in the vanguard, was soon guarding the baggage, which suggests that his 'battle', or division, deployed first while the other divisions passed him to deploy further north. But Geoffrey le Baker hints that the Black Prince's division crossed the Miosson first: *The Prince's section found a narrow ford and crossed the river with carts. They then moved on out of the valley, crossing the fences and ditches, and seized the hill, because of the undergrowth they managed to keep themselves concealed in a strong position, higher than that of the enemy.*[20] As the Chandos Herald put it: *We who were in the rear, should now be in the front.* If this was the case, then it seems probable that the Black Prince envisaged retreating south once again with Warwick in the vanguard.

The English may have feared attack as they marched along the western side of the forest of Nouaillé, and so the Prince stationed archers on his left flank. Certainly the Black Prince dismounted and spoke to the archers shortly after he addressed the men-at-arms. Written sources had made little reference to archers until this point, suggesting that they had suddenly become rather important. Supposedly the Prince said: *Your courage and your faith are well known to me, for in many great dangers you have shown yourselves as not unworthy sons and kinsmen of those who, under the lead of my father and forefathers, the Kings of England, found no labour too impossible, no place too difficult to take, no mountain too hard to climb, no tower too strong*

to win, no army unbeatable, no armed host too great. He then ordered them to stand firm in the hope of rich spoils from the French.

Another explanation of the somewhat contradictory sources suggests that the Prince initially paused near the southern end of the wood but shortly afterwards moved further north.[21] One way or another he positioned his forces along the western and northern sides of Nouaillé wood, where they were largely protected by one or more substantial hedges that ran alongside most of the track. The centre of the Anglo-Gascon position was on a low enclosed plateau at the northern end of the wood while the French camp was out of sight over the brow of a low hill further north.

This gently undulating landscape consisted of woodland, pasture and scattered vineyards belonging to the churches and citizens of Poitiers. However, the broken ground around Nouaillé itself was not typical and provided the best, if not the only, suitable defensive position near to hand. Furthermore the ground selected by the Prince of Wales was broken by vines, other forms of agriculture, very thick hedges, woods, marshes and a stream at the bottom of a relatively steep valley.

Reports by the Captal de Buch's scouts stated that the French King's army was displaying 87 banners, suggesting it was bigger than was really the case. The French camp also seems to have been spread over a wide area. According to Froissart the scouts attacked some stragglers and took prisoners, spreading alarm amongst the French, although in reality Froissart was probably confusing this reconnaissance with another more aggressive move the following day.

Froissart and the other chroniclers do, however, provide important information about the way the Black Prince's men strengthened their naturally defensible position. In Froissart's words: *The English camped therefore in this spot known in the country as the Plains of Maupertius, which they cunningly fortified with thick hedges of thorn, placing all their baggage vehicles well to the rear. In front they dug several ditches, to prevent any sudden attack on horseback.* In Geoffrey le Baker's words: *He surveyed the scene, and saw that to one side there was a nearby hill encircled by hedges and ditches outside* but clear inside, for part of it was pasture and bramble-thickets, part of it planted with vines, and the rest sown fields. In these fields he believed the French army to be drawn up. Between our men and the hill was a deep broad valley and a marsh, watered by a stream. Le Baker also stated that one end of the ditch or hedge 'reached down to the marsh', that the upper part of the hedge was 'well away from the slope', and that the Earl of Salisbury's division was stationed 'a stone's throw' away from it. Furthermore he pointed out that there was a gap in the hedge so that carts could go through it in autumn, perhaps to collect the harvest or gather winter fuel from the forest. Other interpretations of the sources could indicate that there may have been two substantial gaps in the famous hedge. Furthermore it is possible that the often mentioned ditch was partly natural and lay in the valley that sloped down to the Miosson near another ford called the Gué de Russon. The English may have enlarged the ditch, or all these references to ditches might simply relate to field fortifications on the right flank of the Anglo-Gascon line.

The idea that the French remained totally ignorant of the Anglo-Gascon presence seems incredible for, as the Chandos Herald later wrote: *They camped one in front of the other, and were lodged so close that they watered their horses in the same river.*[22] According to Froissart, much credit should go to Lord James Audley: *a prudent and valiant man, and by his advice the army had been drawn up in order of battle.* By the time the battle began, according to Froissart: *The Prince was with the main body of his army among the vineyards, all on foot, but with their horses close by so that they could mount without delay if need arose. On their most exposed side they had placed their carts and other tackle as fortifications, so that they could not be attacked from this quarter.*

In the words of Geoffrey le Baker: *The Earl of Warwick, in command of the vanguard, held the slope down to the marsh.* Clearly English archers were

The town of Chauvigny, with its massive castle, urban fortifications and soaring churches, was a major centre of feudal administration in 14th-century Poitou. It was here that the main part of King John II's army crossed the river Vienne as they overtook the Black Prince's raiders. The Lord of Chauvigny was himself captured in a skirmish at La Chaboterie, two days before the main battle of Poitiers. (Author's photograph)

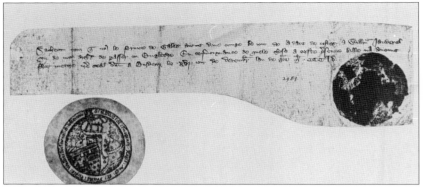

The so-called Jodrell Pass is a remarkable relic of the Black Prince's 1355–56 campaigns. However, it relates to a man who almost certainly missed the battle of Poitiers. It is an official pass, allowing its bearer to return to England, and says in medieval French: *'Know all that we, the Prince of Wales, have given leave, on the day of the date of this instrument, to William Jauderel, one of our archers, to go to England. In witness of this we have caused our seal to be placed on this bill. Given at Bordeaux, 16th December in the year of grace 1355.'* (John Rylands Library, Manchester)

stationed on both flanks though others may have lined the hedge. It is possible that the archers on the extreme left were under the Earl of Oxford's command and that Warwick had others on his immediate right, next to the Prince's division. The English rearguard, under Salisbury and Suffolk, now formed the northern end of the line and also included some German troops. The most significant gap in the hedge was clearly in this area. Here, the right flank of the Anglo-Gascon position was more open and the slope of any 'hill' would have been too gentle to offer much protection. Perhaps here other wagons were used as a field fortification while most of the baggage was concealed within the wood where it would be harder for the French to capture it.

To summarise the final Anglo-Gascon array, the Earls of Warwick and Oxford commanded the left where the ground sloped down to the Miosson. The Earl of Salisbury, supported by the Earl of Suffolk, commanded the right while the Prince commanded the centre. A small reserve of mounted men-at-arms and 400 archers remained in the rear. The Black Prince's army was now in a very strong defensive position with Nouaillé forest immediately behind them; their front being protected by thick hawthorn hedges, scrub and rows of vines. It is worth noting that the brambles mentioned in some sources still exist and, although they are only a few inches high, they cover a large area and make walking – even unarmed and without armour – quite difficult. The English archers had

The famous knightly effigy in Ash church portrays elaborate styles of mid-14th-century armour and military costume. The bascinet helmet has decorated brow and crest pieces, plus pendent scales to give added protection to the sides and back of the head. (*in situ* parish church, Ash, Kent; author's photograph)

their traditional places on the wings. On the right, trenches had probably been dug to protect them, and on the left they were defended by the Miosson and its marshes. Nevertheless, the Anglo-Gascon army remained fearful, hungry, thirsty and outnumbered.

It was said that news of the English presence reached King John II as he was about to enter Poitiers on Saturday, and that he ordered his army to turn around and pitch camp, though it was not until late evening that all were settled. On Sunday morning, 18 September, John and his sons attended Mass in the royal pavilion. The King then summoned his leading barons, advisors and leaders of allied contingents. It was soon agreed that they should unfurl their banners and array for battle. Trumpets were sounded, men-at-arms were armed by their servants, mounted their war-horses and assembled in their *batailles* or divisions. The sacred Oriflamme, held by Geoffroi de Charny, fluttered above all other banners.

The Cardinal of Périgord's peace efforts

Some time during these preparations the Cardinal of Périgord rode up from Poitiers, which he had left early that morning. The French may also have received some reinforcements, perhaps infantry, from Poitiers on Sunday morning. At one point the Black Prince offered to give up the towns and castles he had taken, free his captives without ransoms and not take up arms against the French King for seven years. Such a proposal was a clear indication that he did not want to fight. However, according the Italian chronicler Matteo Villani, the Prince also demanded the King's daughter in marriage with the County of Enghien as her dowry. The French rejected these terms and instead John II proposed that the Prince and 100 of his knights surrender while the rest of the army would be allowed to go home. Finally Geoffroi de Charny proposed settling the matter with a combat of 100 champions from each side, but the less

The Benedictine Abbey at Nouaillé nestles in the valley of the Miosson and is surrounded by low wooded hillsides. It is seen here looking from the north-east. The Black Prince's army would have passed on the other side of the Abbey, hoping to remain hidden from French scouts. (Author's photograph)

romantic Earl of Warwick turned this idea down.

While the Cardinal and his retinue shuttled to and fro, representatives of both armies apparently met between their respective positions. On one such occasion Chandos came face to face with Clermont. According to Froissart both wore the same heraldic device, a Virgin azure, with a sunbeam on the sinister side, embroidered on the surcoats. This resulted in an argument and mutual accusations with the Lord Clermont saying, 'Chandos, how long is it that you have taken upon you to wear my arms?' 'It is you who have mine,' replied Chandos, 'for the arms are as much mine as yours.' 'I deny that,' said the Lord Clermont, 'and were it not for the truce between us, I would show you that you have no right to wear them.' 'Ha!' answered Chandos; 'you will find me tomorrow in the field, ready prepared to defend, and to prove by force of arms what I have said.' The Lord Clermont replied, 'These are the boastings of you English, who can invent nothing new, but take for your own whatever you see handsome belonging to others.'[23] Though only a minor episode of the kind that fascinated Froissart, it nevertheless sheds light on the attitudes and priorities of the English and French military aristocracies.

The *Romance of Alexander*, made in Flanders between 1338 and 1344, includes one of the best 14th-century illustrations of full-sized longbows in use. Here two men are at target practice. It was the rapidity with which these massive bows could be shot that gave them a battlefield advantage over the slower crossbow. (*Romance of Alexander*, Bodleian Library, Ms. Bod. 264, Oxford)

The Cardinal did broker a daylong truce, which enabled both sides to complete their preparations, but eventually his efforts failed and the French ordered him to go back to Poitiers. Both sides blamed the Cardinal for meddling, although the Chandos Herald denied that he had favoured either side. This was not, however, true of everyone in the Cardinal's retinue and as Froissart recorded:

In the Cardinal's company there were brave knights and squires who favoured the French cause more than that of the Prince. When they saw that a battle was inevitable, they stole away from their master and joined the French army, placing themselves under the command of the Castellan d'Amposta, a valiant warrior who was at that time of the Cardinal's household.

It would seem that the French now moved in battle formation to their starting position out of bowshot west of the Anglo-Gascon line. They were in three large *batailles* or divisions, each initially divided into a centre and two wings. The Dauphin Charles commanded the first of the *batailles* with the Lord Douglas, until the Scotsman joined the Marshal Audrehem's mounted division. Since the Dauphin Charles, Duc de Normandie, was an inexperienced teenager, the King placed veterans like the Duc de Bourbon, the Seigneur of Saint-Venant, Sir Jean de Landas and Sir Thibaud de Vaudenay by his side. The Dauphin's standard-

The fortified outer walls and towers of the Abbey at Nouaillé are strengthened by a loop of the little river Miosson. Such protections were designed against bandits and outlaws rather than a full-sized army like that of the Black Prince that appeared outside the Abbey on 18 September 1356. Nor were the monks in a position to refuse to give the Anglo-Gascon raiders any supplies they had available. (Author's photograph)

OPPOSITE Armoured cross-bowmen and men-at-arms in an illustration of King Philip II Augustus besieging the city of Tours or Le Mans. It was made around 1380, but its arms and armour would have differed little from those used by the French at the battle of Poitiers. (*Les Grandes Chroniques de France*, Bibliothèque Municipale, Ms. P.A.30, f. 235v, Lyon)

bearer was Tristan de Maignelay. The second *bataille* was commanded by the Duc d'Orléans and included the King's younger sons Louis and John who similarly had experienced men to look after them. Philip, the King's youngest son, remained by his father's side in the third *bataille*, which was commanded by John himself.

It seems to have been after the French drew up on the slope of a small hill west of the Anglo-Gascon line that King John II sent Eustache de Ribbemont, a veteran of the French attempt to retake Calais in 1351, to make a final reconnaissance of the Anglo-Gascon positions. With him went the highly experienced Seigneurs Jean de Landas, Guichard de Beaujeu and Guichard d'Angle. De Ribbemont came back with an accurate description of the enemy's front line and Froissart claimed that it was Eustache de Ribbemont who proposed the plan of attack that the French King actually adopted. On the other hand it may have been the Scot, Lord Douglas, who first proposed advancing on foot.

Clearly the French faced a serious tactical problem. The English would not attack first and previous experience suggested that they would remain in position for long enough to retreat with honour. If, however, the French attacked, they would lose their only advantage, which was in numbers. It appeared impossible to surround or outflank the Black Prince whereas a direct assault would be on a narrow front, aiming for gaps in the vines and hedges. The Marshal Clermont's advice that the enemy be blockaded and starved into submission resulted in some accusing him of cowardice.

The armies deploy

Despite the difficulties, King John II decided that it was time for a major engagement, perhaps not realising how low the enemy's supplies were. So he abandoned the traditional cavalry assault that had failed at Crécy. Instead he dismounted all except an elite of about 500 fully armoured men, many on armoured horses, selected by the Marshals themselves. Their role would be to disperse the English archers at the start of the battle. Rather confusingly, the Chandos Herald stated that the 400 picked men on armoured horses were led by Guichard d'Angle and Eustache de Ribbemont whom the King begged: *without slackening, to take heed to strike well and spare no pains to break the battle-line.* Perhaps these knights physically led the charges, whereas Clermont and Audrehem were in command, or perhaps D'Angle and De Ribbemont commanded those on armoured horses.

The other men-at-arms, like the mounted infantry, sent their horses to the rear. They would still have to attack uphill, those at the southern end of the battle-line facing quite a steep slope. When the French men-at-arms prepared to fight on foot they shortened their lances to less than two metres (6ft 6ins.) and removed their spurs. The King was reportedly armed with a battle-axe and, having dismounted from his white charger, was dressed in the same 'royal armour' or surcoat that 19 other knights also wore to prevent the King being picked off too easily.

The Marshal Clermont commanded the mounted division on the left, supported by some dismounted men-at-arms under the Constable Gautier de Brienne. Most of the allied German troops under the Counts of Saarbruck, Nido and Nassau also seem have been on the left flank in support of the Marshal Clermont. Marshal Audrehem and Lord Douglas

The junction of the D12 road from Nouaillé (right) and a smaller road (left) leading down to the river Miosson at what had been the Gué de Russon ford, seen here looking north. The road on the left might have been the original Maupertius 'bad track', though the name is now usually associated with La Cardinerie farm, which is a hundred or so metres back along the road on the right. The French army's camp on the day before the battle of Poitiers was probably a kilometre or so away, behind the trees on the right. (Author's photograph)

commanded the French mounted division on the right. The role of the majority of the French crossbowmen is unknown, though their later position suggests that they started out in support of the assault cavalry on the French right, perhaps hoping to counter the numerous archers extending from the English left.

As Froissart stated: *The prince's army was drawn up more or less as the French knights had reported to their king, except that he had ordered a body of wise and brave knights to remain on horseback between his battalions, to withstand the battalion of the French marshals. They had, moreover, on their right flank placed three hundred men and as many archers, all mounted, on a hill which was neither very high nor very steep.* The latter formed a strike-force under the Captal de Buch. On Sunday the Anglo-Gascons strengthened their defences, yet there was widespread mutterings about the Prince's original decision to leave so many men behind to defend Gascony. The English were also unable to leave their positions though they and their horses had access to the river Miosson. During the night before the battle there was, according to the Chandos Herald, skirmishing and the English did not sleep much.

THE OPENING MOVES

The following morning Mass was said in the Anglo-Gascon army, many men were knighted in the field and the Black Prince gave his final instructions. No prisoners were to be taken until after the battle was won, but this did not mean that the enemy was to be slaughtered. Instead the troops should resist the temptation to go searching for wealthy prisoners worthy of ransom.

Froissart may have misunderstood the capture of Eustace d'Aubrecicourt, which forms a chivalric episode in this romantic chronicler's account of the battle. According to him it resulted from a knightly challenge and a combat of champions between the armies before the main battle: *Sir Eustace d'Ambrecicourt* [sic], *being mounted, placed his lance in its rest, and fixing his shield, struck spurs to his horse, and galloped up to the battalion* [of Germans attached to the French side]. *A German knight called*

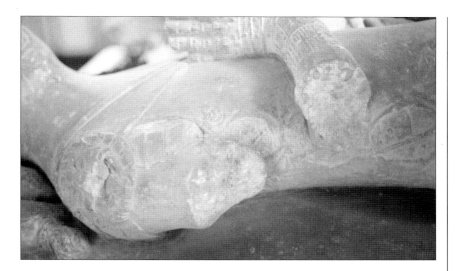

Another detail from the elaborate though damaged English effigy at Ash shows the horizontal iron loops of the knight's coat-of-plates worn beneath a tight-fitting surcoat. It dates from the mid-14th century and its armour would have been typical of that used at the battle of Poitiers. (*in situ* parish church, Ash, Kent; author's photograph)

Lord Louis de Concibras [Ludwig von Recombes] – *who bore for arms five roses, gules, on a shield argent, while those of Sir Eustace were ermine, three humets in pale gules – perceiving Sir Eustace quit the army, left his battalion that was under the command of Earl John of Nassau ... The shock of their meeting was so violent that both fell to the ground. The German was wounded in the shoulder, and was not able to rise again so nimbly as Sir Eustace who, when he had taken breath, was hastening to the knight as he lay on the ground, but five German men-at-arms came upon him, struck him down, and made him prisoner.* The Chandos Herald was more prosaic, recalling that 'as the French book says,' Eustace d'Aubrecicourt was captured while on a battlefield reconnaissance along with the Lord of Curton. Another possibility is that this clash took place at the northern end of the battlefield where cavalry under D'Aubrecicourt might have been creating a diversion while the rest of the Anglo-Gascon army prepared to retreat. The Nassau contingent seems to have taken several prisoners at the

The modern farm of La Cardinerie is popularly believed to have been the site of a farm or settlement called Maupertius in the 14th century. There probably was a farmstead or hamlet here at that time, but the name Maupertius meant 'bad road' or 'bad track' and must originally have referred to a route rather than a habitation. (Author's photograph)

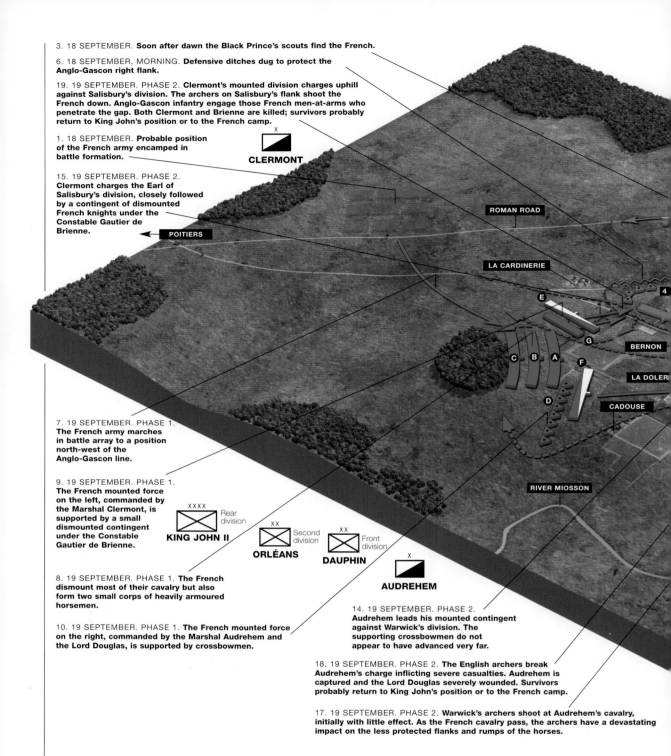

3. 18 SEPTEMBER. Soon after dawn the Black Prince's scouts find the French.

6. 18 SEPTEMBER, MORNING. Defensive ditches dug to protect the Anglo-Gascon right flank.

19. 19 SEPTEMBER. PHASE 2. Clermont's mounted division charges uphill against Salisbury's division. The archers on Salisbury's flank shoot the French down. Anglo-Gascon infantry engage those French men-at-arms who penetrate the gap. Both Clermont and Brienne are killed; survivors probably return to King John's position or to the French camp.

1. 18 SEPTEMBER. Probable position of the French army encamped in battle formation.

CLERMONT

15. 19 SEPTEMBER. PHASE 2. Clermont charges the Earl of Salisbury's division, closely followed by a contingent of dismounted French knights under the Constable Gautier de Brienne.

POITIERS

ROMAN ROAD

LA CARDINERIE

E

BERNON

C B A F

G

LA DOLER

D

CADOUSE

7. 19 SEPTEMBER. PHASE 1. The French army marches in battle array to a position north-west of the Anglo-Gascon line.

9. 19 SEPTEMBER. PHASE 1. The French mounted force on the left, commanded by the Marshal Clermont, is supported by a small dismounted contingent under the Constable Gautier de Brienne.

XXXX Rear division
KING JOHN II

XX Second division
ORLÉANS

XX Front division
DAUPHIN

RIVER MIOSSON

8. 19 SEPTEMBER. PHASE 1. The French dismount most of their cavalry but also form two small corps of heavily armoured horsemen.

X
AUDREHEM

10. 19 SEPTEMBER. PHASE 1. The French mounted force on the right, commanded by the Marshal Audrehem and the Lord Douglas, is supported by crossbowmen.

14. 19 SEPTEMBER. PHASE 2. Audrehem leads his mounted contingent against Warwick's division. The supporting crossbowmen do not appear to have advanced very far.

18. 19 SEPTEMBER. PHASE 2. The English archers break Audrehem's charge inflicting severe casualties. Audrehem is captured and the Lord Douglas severely wounded. Survivors probably return to King John's position or to the French camp.

17. 19 SEPTEMBER. PHASE 2. Warwick's archers shoot at Audrehem's cavalry, initially with little effect. As the French cavalry pass, the archers have a devastating impact on the less protected flanks and rumps of the horses.

BATTLE OF POITIERS – THE FRENCH MOUNTED CHARGES

Morning of 18 September to the morning of 19 September 1356, viewed from the southwest, showing the French camped in battle array, the Anglo-Gascon approach and deployment and the initial French attacks.

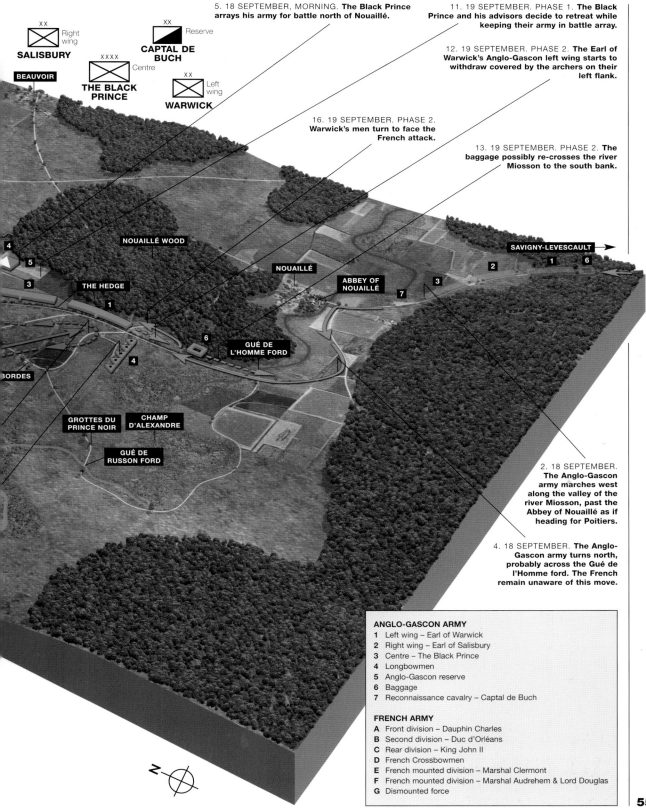

5. 18 SEPTEMBER, MORNING. **The Black Prince arrays his army for battle north of Nouaillé.**

11. 19 SEPTEMBER. PHASE 1. **The Black Prince and his advisors decide to retreat while keeping their army in battle array.**

12. 19 SEPTEMBER. PHASE 2. **The Earl of Warwick's Anglo-Gascon left wing starts to withdraw covered by the archers on their left flank.**

16. 19 SEPTEMBER. PHASE 2. **Warwick's men turn to face the French attack.**

13. 19 SEPTEMBER. PHASE 2. **The baggage possibly re-crosses the river Miosson to the south bank.**

2. 18 SEPTEMBER. **The Anglo-Gascon army marches west along the valley of the river Miosson, past the Abbey of Nouaillé as if heading for Poitiers.**

4. 18 SEPTEMBER. **The Anglo-Gascon army turns north, probably across the Gué de l'Homme ford. The French remain unaware of this move.**

XX **SALISBURY** Right wing

XX **CAPTAL DE BUCH** Reserve

BEAUVOIR

XXXX **THE BLACK PRINCE** Centre

XX **WARWICK** Left wing

NOUAILLÉ WOOD

NOUAILLÉ

SAVIGNY-LEVESCAULT

THE HEDGE

ABBEY OF NOUAILLÉ

GUÉ DE L'HOMME FORD

BORDES

GROTTES DU PRINCE NOIR

CHAMP D'ALEXANDRE

GUÉ DE RUSSON FORD

N

ANGLO-GASCON ARMY
1   Left wing – Earl of Warwick
2   Right wing – Earl of Salisbury
3   Centre – The Black Prince
4   Longbowmen
5   Anglo-Gascon reserve
6   Baggage
7   Reconnaissance cavalry – Captal de Buch

FRENCH ARMY
A   Front division – Dauphin Charles
B   Second division – Duc d'Orléans
C   Rear division – King John II
D   French Crossbowmen
E   French mounted division – Marshal Clermont
F   French mounted division – Marshal Audrehem & Lord Douglas
G   Dismounted force

very start of the battle, including Eustace d'Aubrecicourt, who was tied to a baggage wagon.

The Chandos Herald said that the Black Prince only decided to retreat after his scouts were captured. However, other evidence suggests that the Black Prince had already ordered a withdrawal and that the Earl of Warwick's division at the southern end of the Anglo-Gascon line was already pulling back towards the Gué de l'Homme ford when the French attacked. A withdrawal in the face of the enemy was an exceptionally difficult manoeuvre that required considerable control by the commanders and discipline on the part of their troops.

According to the *French Anonimalle Chronicle*: *On Monday* [the day of the battle] ... *the Earl of Warwick crossed a narrow causeway over the marsh ... but the press of the carriages of the English army was so great and the causeway so narrow that they could hardly pass and so they remained through the first hour of daylight. And then they saw the vanguard of the French army come towards the Prince ... And so the Earl of Warwick turned back with his men.*[24] This would suggest that Warwick's division was unable to withdraw as smoothly as planned. It is also unlikely that this was a feint to prompt the French into a premature attack.

Because of confusion in the sources it is unclear whether all or most of the Anglo-Gascon baggage crossed the Miosson and whether it may have attempted to re-cross the stream later in the battle. What is undeniable is that Warwick's movement prompted the first French cavalry assault. It is almost certain that a substantial body of English archers was positioned further out on the Anglo-Gascon left flank to cover Warwick's withdrawal or that of the baggage wagons. These archers

A track still known as the *Voie Romain* or Roman Road runs through the Forest of Nouaillé, parallel to the modern railway-line about 100 metres (109yds) away. In the 14th century this was the main route between Poitiers and Limoges and it was probably along here that the French expected the Black Prince's army to appear. (Author's photograph)

The well-known Flemish *Romance of Alexander* manuscript, made between 1338 and 1344, includes illustrations of various forms of arms and armour. The style being worn by these two dismounted men-at-arms or knights includes pointed bascinet helmets with mail aventails, coats-of-plates worn over mail hauberks with three-quarter-length sleeves, and full armour for the limbs. (*Romance of Alexander*, Bodleian Library, Ms. Bod. 264, Oxford)

may have been in or next to a marshy area where the valley in front of the Anglo-Gascon line met the river Miosson. As soon as the French cavalry under the Marshal Audrehem advanced, some or all of Warwick's division turned to face this threat. It was now about 9.00am. The battle had begun and would end, except for pursuit and mopping up, around midday.

Movement at the southern end of the Anglo-Gascon line was reported to the French commanders, or at least to the Marshal Audrehem, whose heavily armoured cavalry, perhaps supported by crossbowmen, were facing this part of the Black Prince's array. Audrehem concluded that his enemy was retreating and informed the Marshal Clermont, whose cavalry were facing the northern end of the Anglo-Gascon position. Seeing no movement amongst those in front of him, Clermont doubted that the enemy were withdrawing. Nevertheless, Audrehem promptly led his cavalry against Warwick's division, accompanied by the Lord Douglas and perhaps supported by French crossbowmen, though the latter do not appear to have advanced far. This initial French assault was at first downhill, then uphill against the Anglo-Gascon line.

The Chandos Herald quoted what might well have been the verbatim recollections of French men-at-arms who were involved in these attacks. *Quoth the Marshal d'Audrehem: 'Certes, little do I esteem your trouble. Soon we shall have lost the English if we do not set forth to attack them.' Quoth the Marshal de Clermont: 'Fair brother, you are in sore haste. Do not be so eager, for we shall surely come there betime, for the English do not flee, but come at a round pace.*[25] This led to a quarrel and the accusations of cowardice that seem to have been an almost inevitable feature of such disagreements between senior members of the military aristocracy. Although Clermont disagreed with Audrehem's decision to charge, he felt bound to follow suit and so attacked the other flank, supported by German men-at-arms.

AUDREHEM'S AND CLERMONT'S MOUNTED ASSAULT

Since the archers protecting Warwick's left flank were in marshy or swampy ground, Audrehem's assault cavalry could not reach them and apparently aimed for the main part of Warwick's division as it withdrew. The English archers shot at the advancing cavalry but their arrows could not penetrate the French armour, nor at first their horse armour. Le Baker described the ineffectiveness of the archers' first volleys: *The cavalry … offered the archers as a target only their forequarters, which were well protected by steel and leather plates, so that the arrows aimed at them either shattered or glanced off heavenward,* [to] *fall on friend and foe alike.*

These archers may have been commanded by the Earl of Oxford, or Oxford may have hurried up with orders to move left, further into the marsh. One way or another, these archers were soon able to shoot at the flanks of the French cavalry as it crossed their front. Newer forms of horse-armour, though stronger than the old mail bards, which could easily be pierced by longbow arrows, only protected the heads, neck and

ENGLISH LONGBOWMEN AT THE BATTLE OF POITIERS
(pages 58–59)

The longbowmen of William Montague (1), Earl of Salisbury's division were on the right or northern flank of the Anglo-Gascon position at the battle of Poitiers. One or more comparable units of English and Welsh archers were on the extreme left or southern flank. At the start of the battle these two units of longbowmen played a major role in defeating a cavalry attack by French divisions led by the Marshals Clermont and Audrehem. The cavalry assaults were themselves intended to break up the Black Prince's units of archers so that subsequent attacks by dismounted French knights could get to grips with the similarly dismounted Anglo-Gascon men-at-arms. At first some of the Earl of Salisbury's archers almost certainly had to shoot at a relatively high angle over the famous 'hedge', which formed such a major feature in the Black Prince's defensive position. This hedge was clearly a significant barrier, being much thicker and taller than most modern hedges. Only when the unseen French troops reached the hedge and attempted to force a way through the two recorded gaps in the undergrowth and trees would the majority of archers have been able to aim directly at their enemies. Whereas the Marshal Audrehem's attack against the southern end of the Anglo-Gascon line was repulsed with relative ease, the Marshal Clermont's cavalrymen were closely supported by a line of dismounted French men-at-arms under the Constable Brienne and very nearly broke through. As a result the elderly Earl of Suffolk (2)

brought reinforcements from the centre of the English line to support the younger and less experienced Earl of Salisbury. However, both French assaults were eventually defeated. Clermont and Brienne were killed while Audrehem was captured. In this picture Sir William Montague, Earl of Salisbury, has a steel bascinet with its dog-faced visor raised (3). Sir Robert Ufford, the elderly Earl of Suffolk, is shown here wearing a slightly earlier style of armour, which included a mail coif (4) over a thickly padded arming cap. The fact that many members of the military aristocracy seemingly continued to wear the armour styles of what might be called 'their generation' is indicated by both pictorial and written sources. In contrast the infantry, including the great majority of English bowmen, used whatever armour they could afford or could loot or capture on campaign. Three of the four bowmen shown here each wear slight variations of a basic theme while the fourth (5) has no protection at all. Instead he wears the basic 14th-century western European costume consisting of an unpadded linen coif on his head, a tunic or shirt and relatively tight hose over his legs. Two other bowmen (6 & 7) have close-fitting iron cervelière helmets while the third (8) has a more modern bascinet helmet with a mail aventail attached. Two wear short-sleeved mail shirts that do not inhibit the drawing of their bows, plus in one case a mail coif. The archer in the centre (6) lacks mail but is protected by a thickly quilted gambeson. Meanwhile all the archers have stiff leather bracers above their left wrists to stop their bowstrings causing injury (9). (Graham Turner)

The junction of the D12 road from Nouaillé (left) and a smaller road (right) leading down to the river Miosson, looking south. Immediately beyond the junction is a small hedge that is unlikely to have marked the line of the hedge that featured so prominently at the battle of Poitiers. That was almost certainly the much more massive growth visible beyond the smaller hedge. (Author's photograph)

Some German mercenaries fought in the Black Prince's army in 1356 and a substantial contingent of German allies or mercenaries was found in King John II's army. Their arms and armour would have differed only in detail from that of the English and French, though large surcoats do not seem to have been as popular in German Imperial territory as elsewhere. The 'Guard at the Holy Sepulchre' seen in this carving dating from around 1345 has a coat-of-plates, but otherwise largely relies on mail. (Musée de l'Oeuvres Notre Dame, Strasbourg; author's photograph)

forequarters of the animals. As their unprotected flanks and rumps were exposed, more and more animals were wounded, panicked, threw their riders, refused to advance or galloped from the field. Certainly Marshal Audrehem's cavalry assault was severely disrupted before coming into contact with Warwick's dismounted men-at-arms. The charge was broken and suffered severe casualties, Audrehem being captured. Froissart states that Lord James Audley himself wounded the Marshal Audrehem, and that: *The battalion of the Marshals was soon after put to the rout by the arrows of the archers, and the assistance of the men-at-arms, who rushed amongst them as they were struck down, and seized and slew them at their pleasure.* The Lord Douglas was severely wounded and only escaped because his companions dragged him to safety. Other survivors probably made their way back to King John's position or to the original French camp.

Though unconvinced that the enemy were really withdrawing, Marshal Clermont followed Audrehem's example and attacked the Earl of Salisbury's division. In fact Clermont's advance was less precipitous than Audrehem's and maintained contact with its supporting contingent of dismounted men-at-arms under the Constable Gautier de Brienne. It may also have been launched a little later than Audrehem's charge. Nevertheless, Clermont's men still had to advance up a slope towards a gap or gaps in the hedge. Before reaching this hedge Clermont's and Brienne's divisions were hit by arrows before being blocked by English and Gascon men-at-arms. Geoffrey le Baker provides colourful details: *Nor did the archers fail in their duty but, from a safe position protected by the mound, they attacked those above the ditch and beyond the hedge, aiming arrows which defeated armoured knights while our crossbowmen let fly bolts fast and furiously.* This was one of the few references to crossbowmen in the Black Prince's array, and they were probably Gascons.

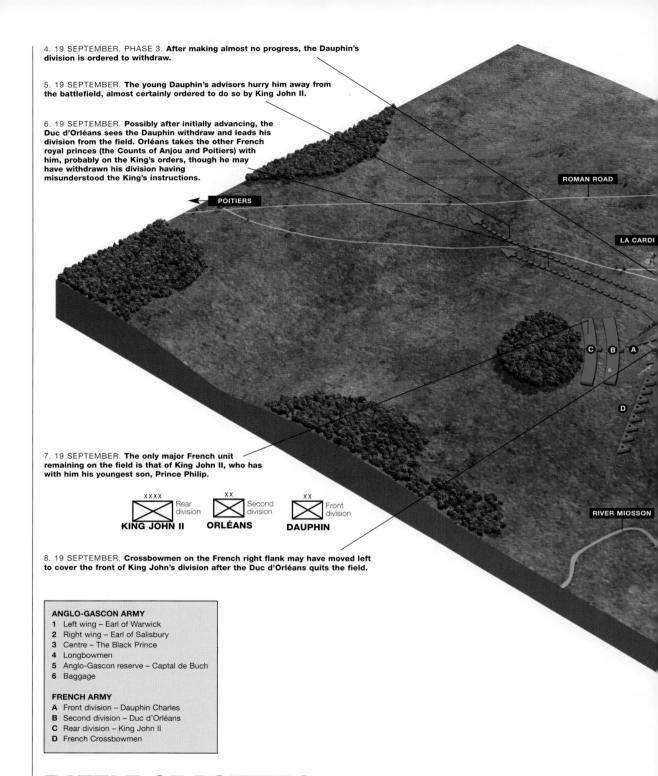

4. 19 SEPTEMBER. PHASE 3. **After making almost no progress, the Dauphin's division is ordered to withdraw.**

5. 19 SEPTEMBER. **The young Dauphin's advisors hurry him away from the battlefield, almost certainly ordered to do so by King John II.**

6. 19 SEPTEMBER. **Possibly after initially advancing, the Duc d'Orléans sees the Dauphin withdraw and leads his division from the field. Orléans takes the other French royal princes (the Counts of Anjou and Poitiers) with him, probably on the King's orders, though he may have withdrawn his division having misunderstood the King's instructions.**

POITIERS

ROMAN ROAD

LA CARDI

C B A

D

7. 19 SEPTEMBER. **The only major French unit remaining on the field is that of King John II, who has with him his youngest son, Prince Philip.**

xxxx
Rear division
KING JOHN II

xx
Second division
ORLÉANS

xx
Front division
DAUPHIN

8. 19 SEPTEMBER. **Crossbowmen on the French right flank may have moved left to cover the front of King John's division after the Duc d'Orléans quits the field.**

RIVER MIOSSON

ANGLO-GASCON ARMY
1   Left wing – Earl of Warwick
2   Right wing – Earl of Salisbury
3   Centre – The Black Prince
4   Longbowmen
5   Anglo-Gascon reserve – Captal de Buch
6   Baggage

FRENCH ARMY
A   Front division – Dauphin Charles
B   Second division – Duc d'Orléans
C   Rear division – King John II
D   French Crossbowmen

BATTLE OF POITIERS –
ATTACK OF THE FRENCH MAIN BODY

19 September 1356, viewed from the south-west, showing the attack of the Dauphin's division and the withdrawal of the Duc d'Orléans, leaving King John II with the only significant French force on the field.

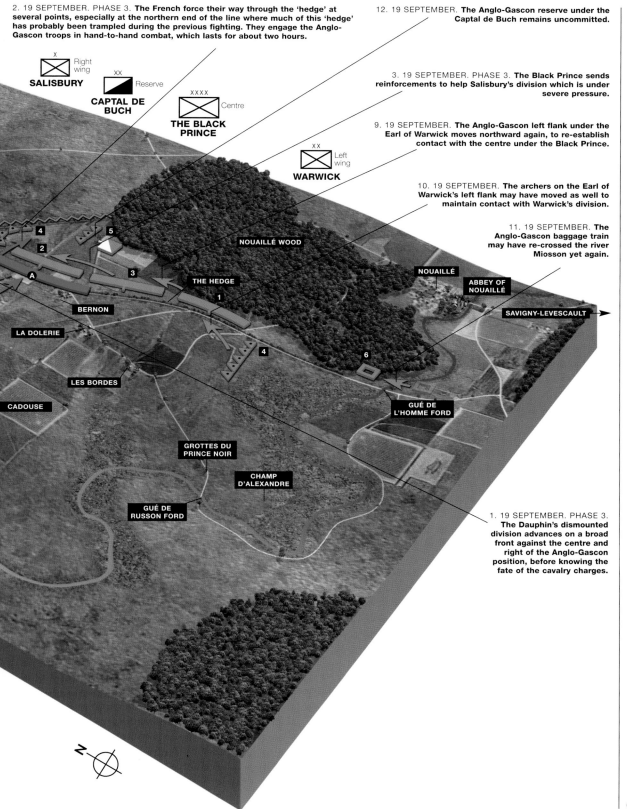

2. 19 SEPTEMBER. PHASE 3. **The French force their way through the 'hedge' at several points, especially at the northern end of the line where much of this 'hedge' has probably been trampled during the previous fighting. They engage the Anglo-Gascon troops in hand-to-hand combat, which lasts for about two hours.**

12. 19 SEPTEMBER. **The Anglo-Gascon reserve under the Captal de Buch remains uncommitted.**

3. 19 SEPTEMBER. PHASE 3. **The Black Prince sends reinforcements to help Salisbury's division which is under severe pressure.**

9. 19 SEPTEMBER. **The Anglo-Gascon left flank under the Earl of Warwick moves northward again, to re-establish contact with the centre under the Black Prince.**

10. 19 SEPTEMBER. **The archers on the Earl of Warwick's left flank may have moved as well to maintain contact with Warwick's division.**

11. 19 SEPTEMBER. **The Anglo-Gascon baggage train may have re-crossed the river Miosson yet again.**

x
Right
wing
SALISBURY

xx
Reserve
CAPTAL DE BUCH

xxxx
Centre
THE BLACK PRINCE

xx
Left
wing
WARWICK

4
2
A
5
3
NOUAILLÉ WOOD
THE HEDGE
1
4
6

NOUAILLÉ
ABBEY OF NOUAILLÉ
SAVIGNY-LEVESCAULT

BERNON
LA DOLERIE
LES BORDES
CADOUSE
GROTTES DU PRINCE NOIR
CHAMP D'ALEXANDRE
GUÉ DE RUSSON FORD
GUÉ DE L'HOMME FORD

1. 19 SEPTEMBER. PHASE 3. **The Dauphin's dismounted division advances on a broad front against the centre and right of the Anglo-Gascon position, before knowing the fate of the cavalry charges.**

N

Froissart recorded: *However, there were some knights and squires so well mounted that by the strength of their horses they passed through and broke the hedge.* The Earl of Suffolk arrived with reinforcements to support Salisbury, and the French suffered heavy losses before being forced back by the superior numbers of English and Gascons. Both Clermont and Brienne were killed and Froissart maintained that the death rather than capture of Clermont: *was owing to his altercation on the preceding day with Sir John Chandos.*

The attack of the Dauphin's division

However, the Chandos Herald suggests that fighting continued until the Dauphin's division entered the fray: *The French book says, and the account is likewise, that the Earl of Salisbury, he and his companions, who were fiercer than lions, discomfited the Marshals and all the barded horses, before the vanguard could be turned and brought across again, for it was over the river* [stream], *but by the will of God and Saint Peter they joined all together and came, methinks, like people of noble bearing right up a mountain until they brought their ranks up to the Dauphin's division, which was at the passage of a hedge, and there, with steadfast will, they came to encounter together.*[26] Here or on the left flank English commanders had to stop their men leaving their positions to strip the dead and wounded on the hillside.

The Dauphin's dismounted division, forming the first line of the main French force, advanced before knowing the fate of the Marshals' cavalry charges and moved against the centre and right of the Anglo-Gascon positions. Though well armoured, the slow pace of the dismounted French men-at-arms led to large numbers being wounded by English arrows. Most reached the hedge and crammed through gaps, which had probably been broadened during Clermont's attack, or broke new gaps to engage the Anglo-Gascon men-at-arms behind.

It is also likely the Dauphin's attack was slightly disrupted by retreating men and horses from the Marshal Clermont's shattered division. Froissart goes so far as to say that some in the Dauphin's *bataille* were overcome by fear following the Marshals' defeat: *Those behind* [in

A battlescene in a French illustrated manuscript from the later part of the 14th century. Both sides consist of fully armoured, dismounted men-at-arms. It was just such troops who did most of the fighting at the battle of Poitiers, where archers, crossbowmen and cavalry played a secondary role. (*Chroniques de France de Saint-Denis*, British Library, Ms. Royale 20.C.VII, f. 13v, London)

Brienne's dismounted corps], *who could not proceed when the rout began, fell back towards the Duke of Normandy's* [the Dauphin's] *battalion which was closely packed in front but which quickly thinned out behind*. However, it may be that Froissart was confusing this with the Duc d'Orléans' withdrawal from the battlefield.

Other sources indicate that the struggle lasted around two hours, and the Black Prince had to send reinforcements to help Salisbury's division, which was under severe pressure. The Duc de Bourbon was reportedly killed and the Dauphin's own standard-bearer was captured, which indicates hard fighting close to the Dauphin himself. The loss of the standard would also have had a serious moral impact and disrupted the cohesion in the Dauphin's division.

Eventually the young Dauphin's advisors recognised they were making no progress and so sounded the retreat. Le Baker makes it clear that the Dauphin's division did not flee but made an orderly withdrawal. Nevertheless, its defeat may have convinced King John II that the battle could not be won. Consequently he ordered the Dauphin and perhaps his other sons in the second *bataille* under the Duc d'Orléans to leave the field since he could not risk their capture.

Once the Dauphin's division was clear of the enemy, he was hurried from the field by his protectors. One English knight, Maurice Berkeley,

could not resist pursuing the French and was captured in the process, though in Froissart's version Berkeley was captured at the end of the battle (see below). Meanwhile the Anglo-Gascons, according to Geoffrey le Baker: *carried those which were wounded of their camp and laid them under bushes and hedges out of the way; others, having spent their weapons, took the spears and swords from them they had overcome; and the archers, lacking arrows, made hast to draw them from poor wretches that were but half dead; there was not one of them all, but either he was wounded or quite wearied with great labour.*[27]

The reasons for what happened next are unclear. Most of the second French *bataille*, which was intended to exploit any English faltering, now abandoned the field. The Duc d'Orléans, seeing the Dauphin leaving, may have thought that it was a general withdrawal and so led his own division off the field, taking with him two of King John's sons, the Counts of Anjou and Poitiers. This is unlikely to have been what the King intended, despite official claims after the battle. Certainly no one believed so. Perhaps it was a misunderstanding, resulting from Orléans' division having already moved some way forward in support of the Dauphin. Or perhaps the retreat of the two Princes and their retinues undermined morale in the rest of Orléans' division. Perhaps the King did order Orléans' withdrawal, while he himself remained to cover their retreat.

Many in the Orléans division did not, in fact, flee. For example Guiscard d'Angle and Jean de Saintré, who had been standing close to the Duc d'Orléans, returned to the thick of the fighting. Some of the Dauphin's closest companions also returned to the battle after escorting the King's eldest son to safety: *'When the Lord Jean de Landas and the Lord Thibaud de Vaudenay who, with the Lord of Saint-Venant, were the guardians of the Duke of Normandy [the Dauphin], they fled with him a good league, they took leave of him and besought the Lord of Saint-Venant not to quit him till they were all arrived at a place of safety, for by doing thus they would acquire more honour than if they were to remain on the field of battle. On their return they met the division of the Duke of Orléans, quite whole and unhurt. Truth it is, that there were many good*

The exterior (RIGHT) and interior (FAR RIGHT) of a late medieval brigandine. Though dating from a century or so after the battle of Poitiers, its construction was essentially the same as the brigandines worn by many infantrymen, and an increasing number of light cavalry, during the 14th century. The exterior is covered with fabric and the numerous rivets that held the internal scales. On the inside these small overlapping iron scales are not covered with fabric. (Warwick Castle Museum; author's photographs)

A stretch of the ancient hedge across the northern end of the battlefield of Poitiers has been uprooted before it meets the Nouaillé to Poitiers road. This means that the surviving hedge can be seen in cross-section as here, showing how deep and dense such ancient hedges could be. It would clearly have formed a major obstacle to men attacking on horseback and even on foot. (Author's photograph)

knights and squires among them, who, notwithstanding the flight of their leaders, had much rather suffered death than incur the slightest reproach.[28] According to Froissart, what remained of the *batailles* of the Constable Gautier de Brienne, the German Earls of Saarbruck, Nassau and Nido, similarly remained with King John; the three German noblemen eventually being killed.

Not surprisingly the Black Prince had difficulty holding his men back from pursuing the Duc d'Orléans since it looked as if the French were in full retreat. Instead there was a short pause and the Prince ordered those men-at-arms who were not otherwise engaged to mount their horses, ready to launch a counterattack. According to Froissart: *They assembled in a body and began shouting, to dismay the enemy, 'Saint George! Guyenne'. It was here that Sir John Chandos spoke those worthy and memorable words to the prince,*

Looking north-west across the upper end of the shallow valley that runs from west of the junction of the Nouaillé to Poitiers road and the probable Maupertius road down to the river Miosson. This valley meets the Miosson downstream from the Gué de Russon ford. The left wing of the French army would have advanced across this depression towards the viewer. (Author's photograph)

Part of the copy of a lost wall painting of the 'Adoration of the Magi' that used to be in St Stephen's Chapel, in the Palace of Westminster. The original painting dated from around the time of the battle of Poitiers and the copy was made by Richard Smirke around 1800, before the Palace of Westminster burned down. This section shows (from right to left) St George with King Edward III, the Black Prince and three of the King's younger sons kneeling in prayer. They wear typical mid-14th-century English armour. (Society of Antiquaries, London)

'Ride forward, sir, the day is yours. God will be with you today. Let us make straight for your adversary the King of France, for it is there that the battle will be decided. I am certain that his valour will not allow him to flee'.

KING JOHN'S ATTACK

Chandos was correct. The only major French unit remaining on the field was now that of King John II. According to Le Baker, John now proclaimed: *Forward … for I will recover the day, or be taken or slain.* King John II advanced towards the Black Prince's division, presumably identifiable by the Prince's banner. Froissart's account now gets rather confusing, suggesting that Gautier de Brienne and the Duc de Bourbon were with the King's division rather than having already been killed: *On one side the Duke of Athens, Constable of France, was engaged with his division, and a little higher up the Duke of Bourbon, surrounded by good knights from the Bourbonnais and Picardy; near to them were the men of Poitou, the Lord of Pons, the Lord of Parthenay, and many more. In another part were the Earls of Vantadour and Montpensier, the Lord Jacques de Bourbon, the Lord Jean d'Artois, and Lord Jacques his brother. There were many knights and barons from Auvergne, from Limousin, and Picardy.* It does seem that the Constable's men were on the right of the French line while the Germans were on the left. The crossbowmen ahead of the right flank may also have moved left to cover the front of the King's division after the Duc d'Orléans quit the field. Clearly they and their *pavesiers* or shield-bearers now advanced ahead of the main body of dismounted men-at-arms.

The French King's *bataille* were the elite of his army and were fresh, though now considerably outnumbered. In fact the sight of this new French division approaching dismayed many in the exhausted Anglo-Gascon line. The Chandos Herald hints that even the Black Prince was taken aback by the French King's unexpected advance: *Looking around him [he] saw that divers had left who had set out in pursuit, for truly they weened that by this time they had accomplished everything; but now the battle waxed sore, for the French King came up, bringing so great a power that it was a marvel to behold.*

French crossbowmen were soon exchanging shots with the English archers. Most of the English archers engaged at this stage were on the

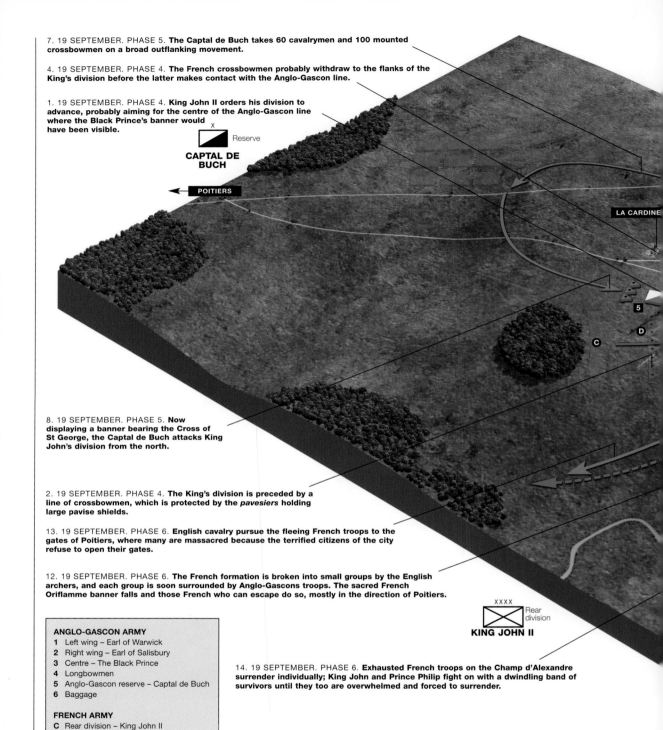

7. 19 SEPTEMBER. PHASE 5. The Captal de Buch takes 60 cavalrymen and 100 mounted crossbowmen on a broad outflanking movement.

4. 19 SEPTEMBER. PHASE 4. The French crossbowmen probably withdraw to the flanks of the King's division before the latter makes contact with the Anglo-Gascon line.

1. 19 SEPTEMBER. PHASE 4. King John II orders his division to advance, probably aiming for the centre of the Anglo-Gascon line where the Black Prince's banner would have been visible.

x

Reserve

CAPTAL DE BUCH

POITIERS

LA CARDINE

5

D

C

8. 19 SEPTEMBER. PHASE 5. Now displaying a banner bearing the Cross of St George, the Captal de Buch attacks King John's division from the north.

2. 19 SEPTEMBER. PHASE 4. The King's division is preceded by a line of crossbowmen, which is protected by the *pavesiers* holding large pavise shields.

13. 19 SEPTEMBER. PHASE 6. English cavalry pursue the fleeing French troops to the gates of Poitiers, where many are massacred because the terrified citizens of the city refuse to open their gates.

12. 19 SEPTEMBER. PHASE 6. The French formation is broken into small groups by the English archers, and each group is soon surrounded by Anglo-Gascons troops. The sacred French Oriflamme banner falls and those French who can escape do so, mostly in the direction of Poitiers.

xxxx

Rear division

KING JOHN II

ANGLO-GASCON ARMY
1 Left wing – Earl of Warwick
2 Right wing – Earl of Salisbury
3 Centre – The Black Prince
4 Longbowmen
5 Anglo-Gascon reserve – Captal de Buch
6 Baggage

FRENCH ARMY
C Rear division – King John II
D French Crossbowmen

14. 19 SEPTEMBER. PHASE 6. Exhausted French troops on the Champ d'Alexandre surrender individually; King John and Prince Philip fight on with a dwindling band of survivors until they too are overwhelmed and forced to surrender.

BATTLE OF POITIERS –
THE ANGLO-GASCON COUNTERATTACK

19 September 1356, viewed from the south-west, showing the attack of King John's division, the Anglo-Gascon riposte and the destruction of the French army.

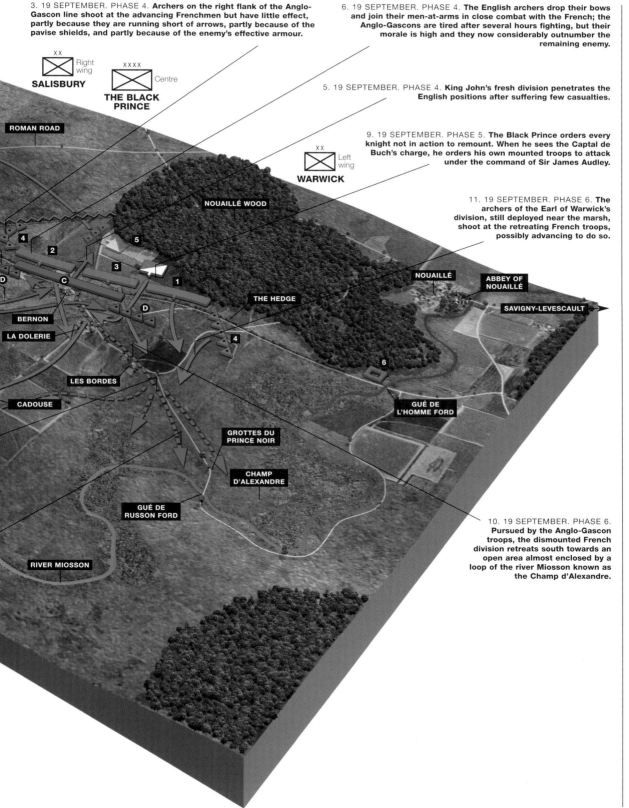

3. 19 SEPTEMBER. PHASE 4. Archers on the right flank of the Anglo-Gascon line shoot at the advancing Frenchmen but have little effect, partly because they are running short of arrows, partly because of the pavise shields, and partly because of the enemy's effective armour.

6. 19 SEPTEMBER. PHASE 4. The English archers drop their bows and join their men-at-arms in close combat with the French; the Anglo-Gascons are tired after several hours fighting, but their morale is high and they now considerably outnumber the remaining enemy.

XX
Right wing
SALISBURY

XXXX
Centre
THE BLACK PRINCE

5. 19 SEPTEMBER. PHASE 4. King John's fresh division penetrates the English positions after suffering few casualties.

9. 19 SEPTEMBER. PHASE 5. The Black Prince orders every knight not in action to remount. When he sees the Captal de Buch's charge, he orders his own mounted troops to attack under the command of Sir James Audley.

ROMAN ROAD

XX
Left wing
WARWICK

11. 19 SEPTEMBER. PHASE 6. The archers of the Earl of Warwick's division, still deployed near the marsh, shoot at the retreating French troops, possibly advancing to do so.

NOUAILLÉ WOOD

4

2

5

3

1

D

C

D

NOUAILLÉ

ABBEY OF NOUAILLÉ

SAVIGNY-LEVESCAULT

THE HEDGE

BERNON

LA DOLERIE

4

6

LES BORDES

CADOUSE

GUÉ DE L'HOMME FORD

GROTTES DU PRINCE NOIR

CHAMP D'ALEXANDRE

GUÉ DE RUSSON FORD

RIVER MIOSSON

10. 19 SEPTEMBER. PHASE 6. Pursued by the Anglo-Gascon troops, the dismounted French division retreats south towards an open area almost enclosed by a loop of the river Miosson known as the Champ d'Alexandre.

71

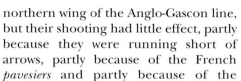

northern wing of the Anglo-Gascon line, but their shooting had little effect, partly because they were running short of arrows, partly because of the French *pavesiers* and partly because of the enemy's armour. Le Baker also noted that the experienced Earl of Suffolk: *Passing through each line, encouraged and urged on individuals, saw that fiery young men did not advance against orders, and that the archers did not waste arrows.* Le Baker provided a dramatic account of the clash: *Then the threatening mob of crossbowmen darkened the sky with a dense mist of bolts, and the archers replied with a hail of arrows from the English side, who were now in a state of desperate fury. Ashwood javelins flew through the air to greet the enemy at a distance, and the dense troops of the French army protecting their bodies with joined shields, turned their faces away from the missiles.*[29] The reference to javelins might be poetic, though it is more likely to suggest that Gascon light infantry were now engaged on the Anglo-Gascon side. Since there is no evidence that the French crossbowmen took part in the subsequent close fighting they probably moved aside to allow the King's men-at-arms to come to grips with the enemy. In fact the French reached the Anglo-Gascon line almost unscathed.

Meanwhile the Black Prince had made his masterstroke by sending the Gascon reserve under the Captal de Buch on a wide flanking movement. They must have set out well before the French King reached the Black Prince's position and Le Baker stated that the Captal's departure made some in the Anglo-Gascon army think he was fleeing. In fact the Captal led 60 mounted men-at-arms and 100 mounted Gascon crossbowmen past the original French encampment. Their ride remained out of sight of the French until they appeared on a small rise behind the left flank of King John's division. The hill around which the Captal de Buch made his flanking attack was for many years afterwards called La Masse des Anglais. As Le Baker described it: *From there he rose up to the battlefield by the path just*

The junction between the Anglo-Gascon right wing under the Earl of Salisbury and the centre under the Black Prince would probably have been on the brow of this hill, as seen from the bottom of the gentle depression that sloped across the English front, down to the river Miosson. The French would have had to attack up this hill, which would have been considerably steeper further down the depression to the right. (Author's photograph)

taken by the French and suddenly burst out of hiding, signalling his presence to our men with the noble banner of St George.

When the Captal's signal was seen, the Prince ordered Sir James Audley to charge with the mounted English men-at-arms, Audley having specifically requested this task. They struck the French King's division before the Captal did so, apparently hitting the Constable of France's men. Since this was probably on the southern flank of the French line it would have had the added advantage of diverting the enemy's attention from the Captal de Buch. The Prince then turned his attention to the German battalion, probably on the left of the French line. Here the Germans were forced to flee, trying to keep out of range of the English archers as they did so. Nevertheless the archers shot down many. As the Germans fled Sir Eustace d'Aubrecicourt was also rescued by his followers under Sir Jean de Ghistelles, since they knew that their leader had been captured by the Germans.

The Prince also had his standard-bearer, Walter Woodland, signal a general advance by the infantry as the last arrows were shot. So the unarmoured English archers threw down their bows and joined in the hand-to-hand fighting. As Le Baker put it: *Armed with swords and shields, they attacked the heavily armed enemy, anxious to buy death dearly since they expected to meet their end that day.* Meanwhile at the southern end of the Anglo-Gascon line the Earl of Warwick had apparently been rejoined by men whom he had detached to pursue the fleeing enemy. The Anglo-Gascon left flank now moved northward in support of the Black Prince.

THE CAPTURE OF KING JOHN II (pages 74–75)
Following the defeat of the first two French attacks at
the battle of Poitiers, and the still largely unexplained
withdrawal of the division commanded by the Duc d'Orléans,
King John II (1) decided to attack the Anglo-Gascon position
with his own division. King John's dismounted men-at-arms
and their supporting crossbowmen were, however, now outnumbered by the Anglo-Gascons and were also struck in the
rear by the Captal de Buch's cavalry flanking attack.
Eventually the King and his surviving followers were forced
into an area called the Champ d'Alexandre at the very
southern edge of the battlefield. Here, in a desperate crush
of struggling men, English and Gascon knights, squires and
common soldiers fought their way to the French King
himself. John II's 14-year-old son Philip (2), the future Duke
Philip of Burgundy, is said to have earned his nickname of
'The Bold' by fighting by his father's side and warning the
older man by shouting warnings such as 'Watch out to your
left!' and 'Watch out to your right!' Then, however, the Royal
standard-bearer Geoffroi de Charny (3) was cut down and
the sacred blood-red Oriflamme banner (4) fell from his
grasp. This marked the end and King John had no choice
but to give up the struggle. The first to ask for the King's
formal surrender was Denis de Morbeke (5), a French squire
from Artois who was fighting for the English after being
banished from France. It is very unlikely that other French
knights 'within their king's gaze' would have surrendered
before King John did so, and the struggle remained intense
until the surviving French men-at-arms realised that their
King had surrendered. The records state that several
French knights were dressed in the same manner as the
King, in an effort to ensure his safety, and in this picture
the French King has, of course, been given the best quality
arms and armour. A gilded bronze crown (6) has been
riveted to the upper part of the dog-faced bascinet helmet
(7); here shown with its visor lowered. A large and thickly
padded mail aventail (8) protects his neck and shoulders,
with cloth-of-gold cords (9) tied through the aventail to the
unseen rondels of shoulder armour beneath. The French
King's rich blue velvet tabard (10) has thickly embroidered
gold thread fleurs-de-lys regularly spaced across its
surface, in what is now called the 'ancient' royal arms of
France. The teenaged Prince Philip has similar armour,
including a typical dog-faced bascinet; here with the visor
raised (11). The wide cloth-of-gold border (12) around the
shoulders, down the openings at the sides, and around
the hem of the Prince's surcoat also serve as a heraldic
indication that the wearer was a youngest son. The arms
and armour of the ordinary knights and foot soldiers of
both sides were much simpler and cheaper. However, in
this picture Denis de Morbeke (5), as a squire from
Artois, has been given armour that reflects the styles
of neighbouring Flanders and the German Empire.
(Graham Turner)

Quite where the Anglo-Gascon baggage train was at this time is unknown, though it may have re-crossed the river Miosson yet again.

THE SLAUGHTER OF THE FRENCH

Once the Captal de Buch struck the rear of King John's division the French line almost immediately collapsed. The wounded Lord Douglas realised that the battle was lost and, in Froissart's words, *saved himself as fast as he could, for he dreaded being taken by the English even more than death.* As the Black Prince and his men hacked their way into the crumbling French formation, the Prince came across Robert de Duras, a nephew of Cardinal Talleyrand of Périgord, *lying dead near a small bush on his right hand, with his banner beside him, and ten or twelve of his people,* as Froissart recorded. *He ordered two of his squires and three archers to place the body upon a shield, and carry it to Poitiers, and present it from him to the Cardinal of Périgord, saying, 'I salute him by that token'. This was done because he had been informed how the suite of the cardinal had remained on the field of battle in arms against him, which was not very becoming, nor a fit deed for churchmen.*[30]

King John's now hopelessly outnumbered division was pushed southwards towards an open area known as the Champ d'Alexandre that was almost enclosed by a loop of the river Miosson. As they fell back the Earl of Warwick's archers bombarded them, breaking up what remained of the French formation. There may even have been archers still positioned in the marsh, shooting at the retreating French troops from the other side. Certainly the French were soon separated into small groups surrounded by English and Gascons. Geoffrey le Baker's description of the resulting massacre remains one of the most graphic in the history of medieval warfare. *Then the standards wavered and the standard-bearers fell. Some were trampled, their innards torn open, others spat out their own teeth. Many were stuck fast to the ground, impaled. Not a few lost whole arms as they stood there. Some died, wallowing in the blood of others, some groaned, crushed beneath the heavy weight of the fallen, mightly souls gave forth fearful lamentations as they departed from wretched bodies.*

Le Baker's appalling account is relieved only by his unreserved admiration for a brave but doomed foe. *Here the Prince was met by a stubborn force of the bravest men. The English were repulsed by the French, whose leader, though of few years, was yet filled with youthful fury and returned all blows with interest, crushing the heads of some, piercing the bodies of others. Everywhere John the pretender went, he gave proof that the Royal House of France was not yet altogether degenerate.*[31]

When the sacred Oriflamme banner fell from Geoffroi de Charny's dying hand, resistance collapsed. Only those on the periphery of the struggle had any chance of escape while King John and Prince Philip fought on with a dwindling band of survivors until they were overwhelmed. Froissart's account of the capture of the King was obviously based upon the recollections of men who were there: *There was now much eagerness manifested to take the King, and those who were nearest to him, and knew him, cried out, 'Surrender yourself, surrender yourself, or you are a dead man!' In this part of the field was a young knight from St Omer, engaged in the service of the King of England, whose name was Denis de Morbeke. For three years he had attached himself to the English, on account of having been banished from France in his younger days for a murder committed during an affray at St Omer. Now it fortunately happened that this knight ... said in good French, 'Sire, sire, surrender yourself.' The king, who found himself very disagreeably situated, turning to him asked, 'To whom shall I surrender myself? Where is my cousin, the Prince of Wales? If I could see him I would speak to him.' 'Sire,' replied Sir Denis, 'he is not here, but surrender yourself to me, and I will lead you to him.' 'Who are you?' said the King. 'Sire, I am Denis de Morbeke, a knight from Artois; but I serve the King of England because I cannot belong to France, having forfeited all I possessed there.' The King thus gave him his right-hand glove, and said, 'I surrender myself to you'.*[32]

Pursuit and ransom

Other exhausted French troops gave themselves up individually, offering items of armour or clothing as token of surrender to captors who then hurried off to capture others. The French looked for men to surrender

to because, in a medieval battle, the captor took responsibility for the safety of his captive. A man who had surrendered was honour bound not to escape but instead to be helpful to his captor. However, this civilised system did not always work as intended. Many years later the Count of Dammartin, who had fought in the King's division, recalled how he had first been captured by a Gascon squire at the battle of Poitiers: *He called on me to surrender, and I did so at once. I gave him my word so that he should protect me. He said that I should be quite safe and need have no fear. Then he tried to take off my bascinet* [helmet]. *When I begged him to leave it, he answered that he could not properly protect me unless he took it off. So he took it off, and my gauntlets as well. As he did so, another man came up and cut the strap of my sword so that it fell to the ground. I told the squire to take the sword, for I should prefer him to have it than anyone else … Then he made me mount his horse and handed me over to the keeping of a man of his, and thus he left me. Then another Gascon came up and demanded my pledge. I answered that I was already a prisoner. So he took an escutcheon from my coat-armour and then abandoned me like the last man. I shouted after him that since he was deserting me I would pledge myself to anyone else who came up and be willing to protect me. 'Protect yourself, if you can,' he shouted back. Another man, who belonged to Sir John Blaunkminster then appeared and demanded my pledge. I answered that I had already been captured by two people, but I gave him my word so that he would protect me. This man stayed with me, guarded me, and eventually brought me to the Earl of Salisbury.*[33] Surrender did not necessarily guarantee safety. The Black Prince was so angry with the captured Castellan d'Amposta, who had been in the Cardinal's retinue before the battle, that he wanted to cut off his head. Fortunately Chandos persuaded the Prince not to do so.

Most of those French who did break away from the rout fled towards Poitiers, pursued by English cavalry up to the gates of the city. Large numbers were cut down because only a few of the fugitives seem to have regained their horses. Froissart recorded the adventure of one French knight who escaped. Sir Edward de Roucy, *not wishing to fall into the hands of the English, had gone about a league off, when he was pursued by an English knight with his lance in the rest, who cried to him, 'Sir knight, turn about, you ought to be ashamed thus to fly!' upon which Sir Edward halted, and the Englishman attacked him, thinking to fix his lance in the target. But he failed, for Sir Edward turned the stroke aside, and with his spear hit his enemy so violent a blow on the helmet that he was stunned, and fell to the ground, where he remained senseless.* Sir Edward then took the English knight prisoner as he fled, and later gained a substantial ransom from him.

Froissart was clearly fascinated by the exploits of those who escaped the catastrophe: *It happened in the midst of the general pursuit, that a squire from Picardy, named Jean de Helennes, had quitted the King's division, and meeting his page with a fresh horse, had mounted and made off as fast as he could. There was near to him at the time the Lord of Berkeley, a young knight who had that day for the first time displayed his banner, and he immediately set off in pursuit of him. When the Lord of Berkeley had followed for some time Jean de Helennes turned about, put his sword under his arm in the manner of a lance, and thus advanced upon his adversary.* In the following combat Berkeley was badly wounded by a sword thrust through both his thighs. Taken prisoner to Châtellerault where his wounds were treated, Berkeley then travelled to the squire's house in Picardy. A year later the young lord was ransomed for enough money to allow De Helennes to become a knight.

These fortunate Frenchmen were in a minority. Outside Poitiers the fugitives found the gates closed against them by the terrified citizens, who feared the English would break into their city. As a result large numbers were massacred. The apparent Anglo-Gascon lack of interest in taking prisoners on this occasion suggests that most were neither knights nor squires worth a ransom, and were probably what remained of the French infantry.

Back on the field of battle the Black Prince was persuaded by Sir John Chandos to attach his banner to a large bush, where it would serve as a rallying point for the Prince's now scattered army. Trumpets were then sounded to recall the soldiers and a small crimson tent was erected for the Black Prince. Meanwhile other English and Gascon soldiers dragged King John II away from Denis de Morbeke. In fact the French King was roughly handled as men quarrelled over him, until he was rescued by the Earl of Warwick and Lord Cobham who took John and his son to the Black Prince's tent.

It was after the hour of vespers before all the English and Gascons returned with their prisoners. In addition to the French King and his youngest son, about 1,000 others 'worthy of ransom' were taken captive and according to Froissart the haul included 17 Counts as well as Barons, knights and squires. Elsewhere it was recorded that several English archers were seen to have four, five and even six men as captives. By the time it was all over the English realised that they had so many prisoners that they decided to ransom most of them immediately.

This seems to have been done in a civilized manner, according to Froissart: *The knights and squires who were prisoners found the English and the Gascons most courteous. Great numbers of them were ransomed that day, or released on their honour to return to Bordeaux on the Gironde the following Christmas in order to pay their ransoms.* The English found abundant booty in the French camp: *It can well be imagined that all those who were with the Prince of Wales in this victorious battle became rich in honour and possession, as much by the ransoms of their prisoners as by the gold and silver, plate and rich*

The open flat country north-east of Nouaillé Forest through which the Captal de Buch and his Gascon men-at-arms, supported by similarly mounted crossbowmen, made their wide flanking movement. The photograph is taken from the now abandoned railway station just east of what used to be the Roman road. The village of Beauvoir can just be seen in the distance on the far right. (Author's photograph)

jewels, and chests stuffed full of heavily ornamented belts and fine mantles. Of armour, arm-defences and helmets they took no notice.

Le Baker's account of the immediate aftermath of the battle was more prosaic: *When the trumpet call had summoned our men together again, they pitched their tents in the cornfields and the whole army at once turned to the care of the wounded, rest for the weary, security for their prisoners and refreshments for the hungry. Realising that some men were missing from their midst, they sent out search parties to find them and bring them back, alive or dead. So if anyone feared for the safety of a missing friend, he hurried to the battlefield to find him, and amongst the heaps of the dead they found them, hardly breathing … Among those half dead and hardly breathing was found Sir James Audley. Placed on a broad shield, and carried reverently by his companions in arms, he was borne to the prince's lodgings.* Next to a hedge for shade, as Froissart wrote, Audley's squires, *disarmed him as gently as they could, in order to examine his wounds, dress them, and sew up the most dangerous.* Sir James Audley handed to his four loyal squires the entire pension that the Prince awarded him for his actions, and when the Prince heard about this he was so impressed that he gave Audley another pension.

The number of ordinary soldiers on the English side killed or wounded in the battle is unknown, and it is only because of the chance survival of a legal document that we know about one such man, William Lenche. He lost an eye and was rewarded by the Prince with rights to the tolls of the ferry at Saltash in Cornwall.

At noon on Tuesday 20 September the Black Prince moved to Les Roches, a few kilometres away, and remained there all Wednesday. The army needed time to get organised for their march, and to sort out their prisoners. They finally set out on Thursday morning, reaching Couhé Verac on the evening of the 22nd. Next day they were at Roffec and then headed down the main road. The Anglo-Gascon return march to Bordeaux was, in fact, quite slow because of their booty and prisoners. They travelled in a compact body, and were preceded by the Earls of Warwick and Suffolk with 500 men-at-arms to secure the road. However, they met no resistance, the whole country being cowed after the battle of Poitiers. The local leadership had been largely wiped out and the French garrisons stayed within their fortifications.

The Black Prince crossed the Charente then turned south-east through Morton (24 Sept.) to Rochefoucault (25 Sept.), then westward to Villebois la Valette (26 Sept.). Somewhere near here part of the army may have taken boats downriver to Blaye on the Gironde. The main force continued on 27 September to Saint-Aulay on the river Dronne. This they crossed on the 28th and marched to Saint-Antonin on the river Isle, which they crossed on 30 September to reach Saint-Emilion. Here some men remained to spend the following winter. The rest crossed the Dordogne on 1 October and on the 2nd most reached Bordeaux. The Black Prince and his retinue, however, waited at Libourne until a triumphal entry had been organised. The Chandos Herald described the subsequent event:

Nobly were they received and welcomed by all the people, with crosses and processions, singing their orisons, all the members of the collegial churches of Bordeaux came to meet them, and the ladies and the damsels, old and young, and serving maids. At Bordeaux was such joy made that it was marvelous to behold.[34]

13 In R. Barber, *Life and Campaigns of the Black Prince* (Woodbridge, 1979) p. 70.
14 In P.E. Thompson (tr. & ed.), *Contemporary Chronicles of the Hundred Years War* (London, 1966) p. 94.
15 Froissart, *The Chronicles of England, France, Spain, etc. by Sir John Froissart*, tr. Thomas Johnes of Hafod, abridged by H.P. Dunster (London, 1906) p.55.
16 In Barber, *op. cit.*, p. 70.
17 From the Register of the Black Prince, in Emerson, *op. cit.*, p. 110.
18 In P.E. Thompson (tr. & ed.), *Contemporary Chronicles of the Hundred Years War* (London, 1966) p. 99.
19 In Thompson, *op. cit.*, p. 100.
20 In E. Hallam (ed.), *Chronicles of the Age of Chivalry* (London, 1998) p. 268.
21 D. Green, *The Battle of Poitiers 1356* (Stroud, 2002) p. 50.
22 Chandos Herald, *op. cit.*, p. 141.
23 Froissart, *op cit.*, p. 56.
24 Green, *op. cit.*, p. 59.
25 Chandos Herald, *op. cit.*, p. 144.
26 Chandos Herald, *op. cit.*, p. 145.
27 In Emerson, *op. cit.*, p. 127.
28 Froissart, *op. cit.*, pp. 60-1.
29 In Barber, *op. cit.*, p. 79.
30 Froissart, *op. cit.*, pp. 59-60.
31 In Hallam, *op. cit.*, p. 272.
32 Froissart, *op. cit.*, p. 64.
33 From the Register of the Black Prince, in J. Sumption, *The Hundred Years War, vol. II; Trial by Fire* (London 1999) pp. 244-45.
34 Chandos Herald, *op. cit.*, p. 147.

THE AFTERMATH

After the carnage of the battle the Mayor of Poitiers proclaimed mourning for the captured King and forbade the celebration of feasts and festivals. To the south, in Languedoc, the États Generaux banned the wearing of gold, silver, pearls, ornamented robes and hats for a year. It was immediately obvious that the battle of Poitiers had been a catastrophe for France. *On that occasion, one could say, the whole flower of French chivalry perished*, was how Froissart summed up the disaster. He maintained that around 6,000 men of all ranks were killed, including 500–700 knights and squires. Modern estimates put casualties closer to 3,000. Many French knights could not be identified because scavengers had removed their clothing before heralds went around the battlefield to identify the fallen. Only the 'identified great' seem to have been taken away for proper burial. The rest were left to rot until the following February when their remains were buried in pits beside the Franciscan church in Poitiers.

'King John II The Good and his youngest son Philip being taken prisoner at the battle of Poitiers', in a late 14th-century French manuscript. The artist has given the King and the Prince the numerous gold fleurs-de-lys on a blue ground which formed the 'ancient' arms of France. The 'modern' arms reduced these fleurs-de-lys to three. The man taking them captive has the quartered arms of England and France, which indicate that he is one of the Black Prince's army. In reality the great majority of knights and squires of both armies would have worn their own coats-of-arms or those of their immediate feudal leaders. (*Chroniques de Jean Froissart*, Bibliothèque Municipale, Besançon)

However, the battle had been a much closer run thing than Crécy. Froissart, like many other chroniclers, also saw it as having been 'more noble' because it was conducted in a properly organised manner. More notable 'feats of arms' had been performed at Poitiers, and French knights certainly had a better chance to demonstrate their valour. Furthermore, King John II did not flee, as his father King Philip VI had done at Crécy. Of those who did quit the field the Dauphin and the King's other sons went first to Chauvigny. These royal princes largely escaped blame, though other senior commanders did not. Some ordinary French knights faced hostility when they got home, the Seigneur de Ferré-Fresnel was dragged from his horse and beaten up by his own peasants who shouted, 'Here is one of the traitors who fled from the battle.' It was a sign of growing disaffection in many parts of France.

In Bordeaux the atmosphere was very different. Here the captured French King settled arguments about who had captured him, and as a result the Black Prince gave Denis de Morbeke 2,000 gold coins, 'to help him maintain his estate'. De Morbeke also received a lifelong pension from King Edward III. When news of the victory reached England, according to Froissart: *There were great rejoicings, solemn thanksgivings were offered up in all the churches, and bonfires made in every town and village.*

Almost forgotten amidst the general rejoicing, the Duke of Lancaster's less successful *chevauchée* in north-western France withdrew to Brittany after being unable to cross the Loire. Thereafter Lancaster, as the English king's Lieutenant in Brittany, contented himself with capturing various castles in Normandy, some of which were sold back to the French for large sums of money. When he heard about the battle of Poitiers, Lancaster returned to England with Philip de Navarre, who had been named King Edward III's Lieutenant in Normandy, leaving Sir Geoffrey Harcourt in charge of English forces in northern France.

In strategic terms King Edward now seemed to have France at his mercy. The French King was his prisoner and within a short time he was to see the Kingdom of France sink into virtual anarchy. Nevertheless, it took the English four years to achieve the peace that the Black Prince's victory seemed to have delivered, and within a decade or so of that peace, these achievements turned into dust in King Edward's hands.

The virtually uninterrupted series of minor victories enjoyed by Anglo-Gascon arms between the battle of Poitiers and the Treaty of Brétigny in 1360 perhaps made King Edward III believe in his initially tactical claim to the Crown of France. In fact this fictitious title remained part of the English Royal Style until George III renounced it in 1801. Nor was the King alone in taking such claims seriously. After Poitiers, many English people felt they could demand anything of the French, and although the Treaty of Brétigny represented a reduction of the more extreme English claims, it remained a disaster for the French

The Church of Saint-Hilaire-le-Grand in Poitiers. The oldest parts date from the 11th century, enlarged and strengthened following a fire in the 12th century. Few survivors of the battle of Poitiers found refuge in Poitiers, a much larger number being slaughtered by the Anglo-Gascon troops outside the city's closed gates. Several months after the battle, some of the dead were, however, brought to Poitiers for proper burial. (Author's photograph)

The depression that protected most of the front of the Anglo-Gascon position at the battle of Poitiers is seen here looking south-west towards the marshes on the northern side of the river Miosson, downstream from the Gué de l'Homme ford. The Marshal d'Audrehem launched the first cavalry assault of the battle across this ground, and King John's shattered division also retreated down this valley as the struggle came to an end. (Author's photograph)

Wooden effigies are now more rare than those carved from stone and they often tend to be very battered. Nevertheless, they can include higher relief detail. Here, for example, a recumbent mid-14th-century English knight has his sword in a scabbard attached to the sword-belt by the new system of two offset loops and rings. This not only kept the weapon at a convenient angle but was also much simpler than the old system of multiple leather laces. (*in situ* parish church, Bures, Essex; author's photograph)

monarchy. On the other hand fear remained that the French would copy the English practice of archery, leading to a ban on the export of bows and arrows in 1357 and 1369. In 1365 archers themselves were forbidden to leave England without a Royal licence.

Within France a general emergency was declared, with the summoning of the *arrière-ban après bataille*. A surviving letter from the Count d'Armagnac, King John's Lieutenant in Languedoc, to the towns in his region announced the defeat and capture of John II: *Dear friends, it is with great sorrow and sadness that I must tell you that eight days ago our lord the King fought against the Prince of Wales, and by the will of God he was doomed to suffer defeat, despite the finest knights who served at his side.*[35] Far away on the north-eastern frontier of France facing the German Empire, news soon reached the Archbishop of Langres and on 14 October he established a commission of four leading citizens to put his town in a state of defence. Langres was far from any threat, yet it was in an area that had only recently been added to the French Kingdom and the local nobility included many with pro-Imperial sympathies.[36]

Before the battle of Poitiers the French King thought that only moral and tactical reforms were needed to face the English threat. After Poitiers the government realised that much more fundamental improvements were required. Despite the failure of dismounted men-at-arms at Poitiers, the French generally adopted these tactics, which they knew as the 'English School'. Abandoning a cavalry charge at the start of a battle, they attempted to develop 'arrow-proof' infantry formations. This was first seen at Nogent-sur-Seine in 1359. Here the dismounted French men-at-arms were still unable to advance, so they tried to turn the flanks of the English archers but again failed. In the end this battle was won when non-noble French armoured infantry attacked the English from behind.

While his father John was a prisoner in English hands, the Dauphin Charles ordered an inventory of all fortified places in France with a view to making them stronger. Historians disagree, however, about the effectiveness of the Dauphin's efforts. Some maintain that there were continuing efforts by French towns to improve their defences, along with a

FRANCE FROM POITIERS TO THE TREATY OF BRÉTIGNY (1360)

The Kingdom of France in 1356.

Territory awarded to King Edward III of England by the abortive Treaty of London (1359).

Territory awarded to King Edward III of England by the Treaty of Brétigny (1360), including lands already held by the King of England at the start of the Hundred Years War.

Imperial frontier territory ruled by French feudal lords.

Provence under an Angevin dynasty as part of the Kingdom of Naples.

Navarrese domains, including those inside the Kingdom of France following Anglo-Navarrese occupations (October 1356–January 1358).

Kingdom of England in 1360.

Papal territory of Avignon, within the Kingdom of France.

Béarn (declared an independent sovereign state in 1347).

Major area affected by the Jacquerie uprisings.

Regions particularly affected by the mercenary 'companies'.

Anglo-Gascon and Navarrese operations.

French and allied operations.

4. 1360: French naval attack on Winchelsea.

9. November 1359–April 1360: Offensive by King Edward III.

5. December 1356: Pont-Audemer taken by the forces of the French Dauphin, future King Charles V. November 1357: Retaken by English.

6. 1357–59: Anglo-Navarrese offensive including the siege of Paris.

3. October 1356–July 1357: English troops and their Breton supporters under the Duke of Lancaster and John de Montfort unsuccessfully besiege Rennes, whose garrison is commanded by Bertrand de Guesclin.

6a. October 1357–January 1358: Anglo-Navarrese occupation of large parts of Normandy and northern France.

7. 29 June–31 July 1358: Army of the Dauphin Charles besieges rebels and their Anglo-Navarrese supporters around Paris.

1. Late September 1356: The Duke of Lancaster withdraws from Angers to Brittany.

2. 29 September 1356: The Dauphin Charles enters Paris and starts to establish a new French government now that his father, King John II, is a prisoner in English hands in Bordeaux.

8. 1359: Raid by Sir John Knolles.

ENGLAND · London · Dover · Winchelsea · Calais · Bruges · Ghent · FLANDERS · 'IMPERIAL' FLANDERS · Lille · 'THE THREE CASTLERIES' · ARTOIS · Cambrai · PONTHIEU · Amiens · PICARDY · THE EMPIRE · Guernsey · Jersey · Pont-Audemer · NORMANDY · Argentan · Paris · BAR · Chartres · Troyes · MAINE · ORLÉANAIS · Rennes · Le Mans · Orléans · BRITTANY · ANJOU · BURGUNDY (French Duchy) · Dijon · Angers · Tours · NIVERNAIS · TOURAINE · Bourges · Nevers · BERRY · Bourbon · BURGUNDY (Imperial County) · POITOU · BOURBONNAIS · Mâcon · SAVOY · Poitiers · MARCHE · La Rochelle · ANGOUMOIS · Saintes · Angoulême · Limoges · LYONNAIS · SAINTONGE · LIMOUSIN · AUVERGNE · Lyons · Bay of Biscay · PERIGORD · Périgueux · St Flour · VELAY · Le Puy · DAUPHINÉ · Bordeaux · GUYENNE · VALENCE · AGENAIS · QUERCY · ROUERGUE · GEVAUDAN · GASCONY · Avignon · PROVENCE · ARMAGNAC · Montpellier · Arles · BÉARN · ASTARAC · Toulouse · LANGUEDOC · Marseilles · CASTILE · SOULE · BIGORRE · COMINGES · FOIX · Narbonne · NAVARRE · ROUSSILLON · Mediterranean Sea · ARAGON

0   100 miles
0   100 km

This magnificent and almost undamaged stained-glass window illustrates several generations and members of the Clare family, who were a powerful aristocratic clan in 14th-century England. The figures seen here also have the sort of arms, armour and military clothing that would have been seen at the battle of Poitiers. (*in situ* Abbey, Tewkesbury; author's photograph)

'King Philip II Augustus of France and his army landing at Acre during the Third Crusade', in a manuscript illuminated around 1380 by Perrin de Cerf. Although the artist has clearly exaggerated the way the King and his followers are bunched together, maintaining a very close formation was an essential tactic when 14th century men-at-arms were fighting on foot or on horseback. (*Les Grandes Chroniques de France*, Bibliothèque Municipale, Ms. 880, f. 256v, Lyon)

significant increase in other sorts of fortification including church towers, bridges, monasteries and manor houses. Others claims that French towns spent very little on their defences between 1356 and 1360 because this was still a period of economic distress following the Black Death.

Politically the impact of the battle of Poitiers was undeniably disastrous. The relative unity of the state was shattered, the reputation of its military aristocracy was tarnished and the young Dauphin Charles found himself trying to rule a realm that had lost a quarter of its territory. This period also saw confusion in matters of loyalty and treason, though it became easier once the Dauphin Charles was proclaimed Regent in March 1358.

Many of these stresses and strains are apparent in the *Complainte sur la bataille de Poitiers*, which was discovered in a legal register in Paris. This laid blame on the shoulders of the nobility, and asked for God's help to the King and his son Philip who were still prisoners in English hands. It reflected attitudes seen amongst the Jacquerie rebels around Paris whose nickname stemmed from 'Jacques Bonhomme' – the archetypal common man of 14th-century France: *The very great treason that they long time concealed, was in the said host very clearly revealed.* The *Complainte* concluded that good men of great courage would avenge Poitiers and bring back the King, who: *If he is well advised he will not forget to lead Jacque Bonhomme and all his great company who do not run from war to save their lives!* Similarly *Le Confort d'Ami* written for King Charles of Navarre by Guillaume de Machaut, and the *Tragicum Argumentum* written by the Benedictine monk François de Montebelluna, similarly bemoaned the shame and dishonour brought upon France.

Fully armoured men-at-arms on horseback, in a Flemish manuscript dating from between 1338 and 1344. One horse has a cloth caparison, probably covering hardened leather or iron armour over its head, upper-neck and breast. The leading horse clearly has these head and neck protections, plus a substantial piece of horse-armour on its chest. Such chest defences are illustrated more clearly elsewhere in the manuscript. (*Romance of Alexander*, Bodleian Library, Ms. Bod. 264, Oxford)

By 1357 a crisis of law and order led to a French Royal Ordnance that permitted peasants to take up arms against brigands and others 'troubling' their area. Previously peasants had been banned from taking the law into their own hands. For the first time they were similarly permitted to 'gather together' to face such threats. Even more serious, perhaps, was the 'rise of the Companies' or contingents of independent or freebooting soldiers who, within two years, were causing devastation in many parts of France.

On a more positive note the Dauphin Charles showed his qualities as a ruler while his father the King was a prisoner. After arriving in Paris as Lieutenant General of the kingdom, he summoned the États Generaux. This was a courageous thing to do as the Estates had a reputation for causing problems for French rulers. Etienne Marcel, provost of the Paris merchants, had, for example, previously demanded that the Estates rather than the King control taxation. Indeed Etienne Marcel was soon causing trouble. Supported by the bishop of Laon, he disputed the authority of the King's counsellors, demanded the release of King Charles of Navarre and seemed likely to choose Charles as King of France. In fact Charles was released and for a while became the master of Paris. After an attempt was made on the Dauphin's life, the Dauphin left Paris and summoned the États Generaux to meet at Compiègne where he planned to retake Paris from Charles of Navarre and Etienne Marcel.

Meanwhile much of the region around Paris was caught up in the Jacquerie rebellion. This was not simply a peasants' revolt, since many of those involved were not agricultural labourers but included craftsmen and even minor officials. To resist the Dauphin, Etienne Marcel joined forces with the Jacqueries, but this caused King Charles of Navarre to change sides and he joined the rest of the aristocratic elite in crushing the Jacquerie. The Dauphin then besieged Paris. Etienne Marcel asked for English help and consequently lost popular support, being murdered by his own followers on 31 July 1358.

After the defeat of Etienne Marcel, the Dauphin Charles became the recognised leader of the country. This was followed by spontaneous uprisings against the English in many parts of France. However, wrangling over King John's ransom caused King Edward to invade northern France in 1359 with an army of 4,000 men-at-arms and 5,000 mounted archers. He had hoped to take Reims where he wanted to be crowned King of France. However, the invasion failed and King Edward temporarily abandoned his claim to the French throne in return for undisputed authority in those lands already held by the English. The result was the Treaty of Brétigny in April 1360.

Under an earlier peace agreement, the Treaty of London in 1359 which never came into force, King John had agreed to give up the entire Atlantic coast of France. Under the Treaty of Brétigny, Edward got Guyenne, Limousin, Périgord, Rouergue, Angoumois and Saintonge. He also kept Calais to which was added Montreuil, Guise and Ponthieu. Furthermore, Edward was freed from his feudal oath to the King of France in respect of these territories. A ransom of 3,000,000 *ecus* was agreed for King John II, to be paid over six years, and as a guarantee John's sons became hostages in English hands. These massive concessions were supposed to be the price of a durable peace. In reality they achieved no more than a truce in what became a very long struggle – the Hundred Years War.

35 F. Autrand, 'La Déconfiture. La bataille de Poitiers (1356) à travers quelques textes français des XIVe et XVe siècles', in P. Contamine (et al. eds.), *Guerre et Société en France, en Angleterre et en Bourgogne XIVe-XVe siècle* (Lille 1991)p. 92.

36 O. Wilsdorf-Colin, 'La mise en défence des Langres au lendemain de la bataille de Poitiers 1356),' in N. Coulet & O. Guyotjeannin (eds.), *La Ville au Moyen Age: Ville et Espace* (Paris 1998) pp. 167-179.

THE BATTLEFIELD TODAY

The Black Prince's *chevauchée* of 1356 took his army through the provinces covered by no less than five Michelin regional Green Guides,[37] so any attempt by a modern battlefield explorer to follow in his footsteps would be quite ambitious. However, the Black Prince's route is very accessible, except for a short stretch when the Anglo-Gascon raiders left the main roads and headed through forests south of Châtellerault. Much of this area now forms part of the Forêt de Moulière and, north of the village of Charasse, none of the existing minor roads runs in the direction taken by the Prince.

The Black Prince's route, and the counter-march of King John II, went through some of the most delightful, fertile and gentle landscape in France. Although the Anglo-Gascons set out from Bergerac on the lower reaches of the Dordogne river, they headed north rather than into the spectacular gorges favoured by modern tourists further upstream. An amateur historian following in their footsteps would be advised to focus on the superb medieval architecture and even more superb food of these regions rather than on looking for magnificent views. A medieval army was, of course, very concerned about the presence of castles and fortified towns, as well as the availability of food. Furthermore it would have been anxious to avoid mountainous terrain wherever possible.

Despite an apparent lack of spectacular scenery, this part of France is well endowed with hotels, guesthouses and well-equipped campsites of all grades, and of course with restaurants. In fact the French domestic tourist has long appreciated these regions. The university city of Poitiers naturally has plenty of hotels in all categories and there is also a good hotel in the village of Nouaillé. Well recommended *chambres d'hôtes* guesthouses can be found in the nearby villages of Roches-Prémarie and Fleuré, while other unlisted guesthouses exist elsewhere. There is a campsite with good facilities in Poitiers and another at Bonnes, north of Chauvigny in the beautiful valley of the river Vienne. The gastronomic specialities of this area seem endless though Poitevan chicken, wildfowl from the forest cooked in various ways, and the nougat of Poitiers must head the list. This is, however, no longer the wine-growing area that it was in the 14th century. Instead Poitou is now famous for its fruit, and many of the locals are especially proud of their cider.

Men-at-arms and infantrymen, including a fully armoured longbow archer, a crossbowman and a *pavesier*, assault a fortified city in a mid- to late 14th-century French manuscript. The only real difference between these soldiers and those at the battle of Poitiers is the cut of their surcoats and the fact that their helmets have rounded rather than pointed 'dog-faced' visors. (*Chroniques de France de Saint-Denis*, British Library, Ms. Royale 20. C.VII, London)

The Barbican and Clock Tower of Warwick Castle. This was the power-base of Thomas Beauchamp, Earl of Warwick, who commanded the Anglo-Gascon left wing at the battle of Poitiers. A number of the most senior French prisoners taken at Poitiers were kept in Warwick Castle. (Author's photograph)

The battlefield of Poitiers or Maupertius is fully accessible and is marked by a small memorial erected 600 years after the event in 1956. The nearby village of Nouaillé is a pleasant dormitory settlement for the large and industrialised city of Poitiers and is still dominated by the restored but imposing Benedictine Abbey. Its small village square has the inevitable café and small shops; the sleepy Miosson stream laps the outer walls of the Abbey and the whole scene is dominated by wooded hillsides. The Abbey itself partly dates from the 12th century and also has an imposing 15th-century dormitory whose tower offers a superb view of the valley.

The main, though still small, D12 road from Nouaillé to Poitiers goes up the hill through the Forest of Nouaillé and, some way after leaving the woods and emerging on to the open undulating plateau, is joined by a smaller road from the left. This was the track, probably the original Maupertius, which ran down to the Miosson, which is now crossed by a small bridge at what had been the Gué de l'Homme ford. This minor road then follows the southern bank of the Miosson back to Nouaillé village.

The tiny hamlet of Les Bordes lies just to the west of this presumed Maupertius road and probably marks the spot of a medieval farmstead. The only way down to the Gué de Russon from Les Bordes is now a private farm track. However, the area known as the Champ d'Alexandre west of the bridge, which marks the Gué de l'Homme ford, is open to the public and includes a small cave or grotto popularly associated with the Black Prince (Les Grottes du Prince Noir).

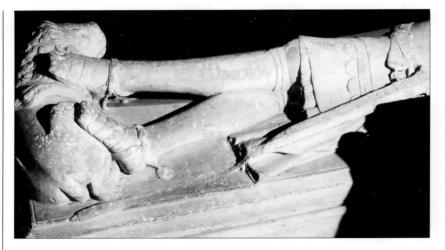

When fighting on foot, knights removed their spurs, as the French men-at-arms were recorded doing before the battle of Poitiers. As spurs were a symbol of knightly rank they would, of course, be shown on the carved effigies that still cover the tombs of knights in many medieval English parish churches. This mid-14th-century example also shows the fully plated greaves that protected the legs, and the overlapping lames of the sabatons that protected the feet. (*in situ* parish church, Ifield, Sussex; author's photograph)

East of the D12, a few hundred metres before it is joined by the presumed Maupertius at a small memorial, another minor road branches off towards Beauvoir and the main N147 trunk road. This does a sharp right and then left turn past a now disused railway station and over the railway itself. The ancient Roman road lay parallel to this railway and at the time of the battle of Poitiers it still served as the main route from Poitiers to Limoges. Today it is marked only by farm and forest tracks. The route taken by the Captal de Buch's flanking attack went across fields and around small copses and cannot be followed exactly. The site of the French camp before the battle would have been just east of, or partly beneath, the modern railway line.

About 200 metres (219yds) south of the junction of the D12 and the presumed Maupertius road to Les Bordes and the Gué de l'Homme, there is still a massive hedge running almost from the D12 to the Maupertius track. Other comparably dense and ancient stretches of hedge exist to the south, close to the Maupertius, and just west of that road. Here their line suggests that there may originally have been an almost continuous hedge from the D12 to the lower slope of a small hill identified only by its height – 134 metres (440ft).

To call these masses of undergrowth and trees 'hedges' is, however, potentially misleading for an English reader. They are more like extended lines of forest and in late summer the huge gnarled apple trees embedded in these hedges still bear fruit. Perhaps apples were there in September 1356, to refresh the Anglo-Gascon soldiers as they awaited the next French attack. The vineyards mentioned by chroniclers of the battle of Poitiers may have gone, but walking across the head of the narrow valley that King John's soldiers had to pass before reaching the Anglo-Gascon line is still difficult because of the matted brambles lurking at ankle height in the unmown grass.

Standing beside these ancient hedges today it is difficult to imagine that almost six and a half centuries ago this was the site of one of the hardest-fought battles of the Hundred Years War.

37 Pyrénées Aquitaine; Périgord Quercy; Berry Limousin; Châteaux de la Loire; Poitou Vendée Charentes.

BIBLIOGRAPHY

Allmand, C.T., *Society at War: The Experience of England and France during the Hundred Years War* (Woodbridge, 1998)

Allmand, C.T., *The Hundred Years War: England and France at War c.1300–c.1400* (Cambridge, 1988)

Ashley, W., *Edward III and his wars, 1327–1360* (1997, reprinted 1993)

Autrand, F., 'La deconfiture, La bataille de Poitiers (1356) …,' in P. Contamine (ed.), *Guerre et Société en France, en Angleterre et en Bourgogne XIVe–XVe Siècle.* (Lille, 1991) pp. 93–122.

Ayton, A., *Knights and Warhorses: Military Service and the English Aristocracy under Edward III* (Woodbridge, 1994)

Barber, R., *Edward, Prince of Wales and Aquitaine* (London, 1982)

Barnie, J.E., *War in Medieval Society; Social Values and the Hundred Years War 1337–99* (London, 1974)

Bartlett, C., & G. Embleton, 'The English Archer, c.1300–1500,' in *Military Illustrated Past & Present*, I (June–July 1980) 10–17, II (August–September 1980) 14–21.

Bennett, M., 'The Development of Battle Tactics in the Hundred Years War,' in A. Curry & M. Hughes (eds.), *Arms, Armies and Fortifications in the Hundred Years War* (Woodbridge, 1994) 1–22.

Broome, D.M., *The Ransom of John II, King of France, 1360–1370* (London, 1926).

Burley, S.J., 'The Victualling of Calais, 1347–65,' *Bulletin of the Institute of Historical Research*, XXXI (1958) 49–57.

Burne, A.H., *The Crécy War: A Military History of the Hundred Years War from 1337 to the peace of Brétigny, 1360* (London, 1955)

Chazelas, A., *Documents Relatifs au Clos de Galees de Rouen …* (Paris 1977–78)

Chevalier, B., 'Pouvoir royale et pouvoir urbains à Tours pendant la Guerre de Cent Ans,' *Annales de Bretagne*, LXXXI (1974) 365–392 & 681–707.

Contamine, P., 'Consomation et demande militaire en France et en Angleterre, XIIIe–XVe siècles', in *Domanda e consumi. Livelli e strutture (nei secoli XIII–XVIII). Atti della 'Sesta settimana di studio' (27 aprile–3 maggio 1974). Istituto inetrnazionale di Storia economica 'F. Datini'* (Prato-Firenze, 1978) 409–428.

Contamine, P., (ed.), *La Noblesse au Moyen Age, XIV–XVe siècles* (Paris, 1976)

Contamine, P., *Guerre, État et Société a la Fin du Moyen Age* (Paris, 1972)

Devries, K., *Infantry warfare in the early fourteenth century* (Woodbridge, 1996)

Devries, K., *Military Campaigns of the 100 Years War* (Woodbridge, 2000)

Dupuy, M., *Le Prince Noir* (Paris, 1970)

Emerson, B., *The Black Prince* (London, 1976)

Fowler, K.A., *The Age of Plantagenet and Valois: The Struggle for Supremacy 1328–1498* (London, 1967)

Fowler, K.A., *The King's Lieutenant, Henry of Grosmont, First Duke of Lancaster 1310–1361* (London, 1969)

Given-Wilson, C., *The English Nobility in the Later Middle Ages: The Fourteenth Century Political Community* (London, 1996)

Goller, K.H., 'War and Peace in the Middle English Romances and Chaucer', in B.P. McGuire (ed.), *War and Peace in the Middle Ages* (Copenhagen, 1987) 118–145.

Green, D., *The Battle of Poitiers 1356* (Stroud, 2002)

Hallam, E.M., *Chronicles of the Age of Chivalry* (London, 1989)

Hewitt, H.J., *The Black Prince's Expedition of 1355–1357* (Manchester, 1958)

Hewitt, H.J., *The Organisation of War under Edward III* (Manchester, 1966)

Jarousseau, G., 'Le guet, l'arrière-guet at la garde en Poitou pendant la guerre de Cent Ans,' *Bulletin de la Société des Antiquaires de l'Ouest* (1965) 159–202.

Jeanjean, J-F., *La Guerre de Cent Ans en Pays Audois. Incursion de prince Noire en 1355* (Carcassonne, 1946)

Johnson, P., *The Life and Times of Edward III* (London, 1973)

Jones, M., 'War in Fourteenth Century France,' in A. Curry & M. Hughes (eds.), *Arms, Armies and Fortifications in the Hundred Years War* (Woodbridge, 1994) 103-120.

Labarge, M.W., *Gascony: England's First Colony 1204–1453* (London, 1980)

Lot, F., *L'Art Militaire et les Armées au Moyen Age* (Paris, 1946)

Lyon, B.D., *From Fief to Indenture: The Transition from Feudal to Non-Feudal Contract in Western Europe* (Cambridge, Mass., 1957)

Ormrod, W., *The Reign of Edward III* (London, 1999)

Prestwich, M., *Armies and Warfare in the Middle Ages: The English Experience* (New Haven, 1996)

Prestwich, M., *The Three Edwards: War and State in England 1272–1377* (London, 1981)

Prince, A.E., 'The Indenture System under Edward III,' in J.G. Edwards (ed.), *Historical Essays Presented to James Tait* (Manchester, 1933)

Rogers, C., *Cruel War and Sharp: English Strategy under Edward III 1327–1360* (Woodbridge, 2000)

Rogers, C., *The Wars of Edward III: Sources and Interpretations* (Woodbridge, 1999)

Sumption, J., *The Hundred Years War, Vol. II Trial by Fire 1347–1364* (London, 1999)

Thompson, P.E. (ed. & tr.,), *Contemporary Chronicles of the Hundred Years War* (London, 1966)

Tourneur-Aumont, J.M., *La bataille de Poitiers (1356) et la construction de la France* (Paris, 1940)

Tout, T.F., 'Some Neglected Fights between Crecy and Poitiers', in *The Collected Papers of Thomas Frederick Tout* (Manchester, 1934)

Wright, N., *Knights and Peasants: The Hundred Years War in the French Countryside* (Woodbridge, 1998)

INDEX

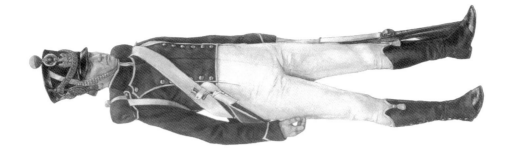

OSPREY
PUBLISHING

FIND OUT MORE ABOUT OSPREY

❏ Please send me the latest listing of Osprey's publications

❏ I would like to subscribe to Osprey's e-mail newsletter

Title / rank

Name

Address

City / county

Postcode / zip   state / country

e-mail

CAM

I am interested in:

❏ Ancient world
❏ Medieval world
❏ 16th century
❏ 17th century
❏ 18th century
❏ Napoleonic
❏ 19th century

❏ American Civil War
❏ World War 1
❏ World War 2
❏ Modern warfare
❏ Military aviation
❏ Naval warfare

Please send to:

USA & Canada:
Osprey Direct USA, c/o MBI Publishing, P.O. Box 1,
729 Prospect Avenue, Osceola, WI 54020

UK, Europe and rest of world:
Osprey Direct UK, P.O. Box 140, Wellingborough,
Northants, NN8 2FA, United Kingdom

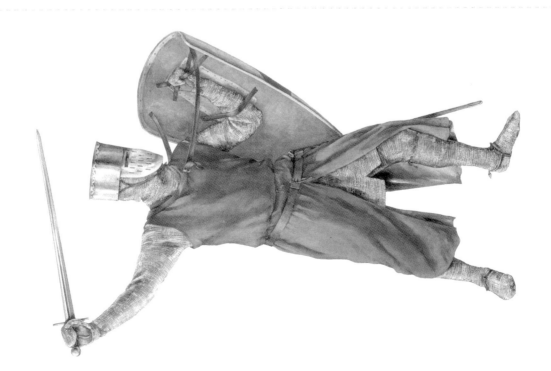

OSPREY
PUBLISHING

www.ospreypublishing.com

call our telephone hotline
for a free information pack

USA & Canada: 1-800-826-6600
UK, Europe and rest of world call:
+44 (0) 1933 443 863

Young Guardsman
Figure taken from *Warrior 22:
Imperial Guardsman 1799–1815*
Published by Osprey
Illustrated by Richard Hook

Knight, c.1190
Figure taken from *Warrior 1: Norman Knight 950 – 1204 AD*
Published by Osprey
Illustrated by Christa Hook

POSTCARD